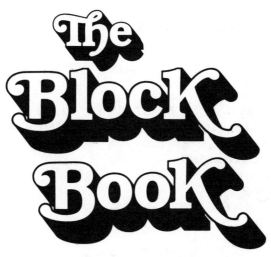

The Block Book

Revised Edition

Elisabeth S. Hirsch
Editor

National Association for
  the Education of Young Children
Washington, D.C.

Book design: Melanie Rose White

Photographs

Judy Burr *132*
Paul Cryan *cover*
Ellen Galinsky *4, 8, 13, 54, 57, 58, 69, 72, 82, 89,
    99, 108, 111, 116, 126, 140, 145, 172, 180, 194,
    195, 196, 197*
Marian Greenwood *199*
Antoinette Grimes *135, 200*
Lois Lord *162*
Marietta Lynch *64, 105, 174, 198*
Lois Main *53, 157*
Merrie L. Murray *123*

Drawings

Susan Hirsch, Chapter 8: pp. 175, 178, 181, 189, 190,
    Appendix 2
Harriet M. Johnson, Chapter 2: "The Art of Blockbuilding,"
    used by permission of Bank Street College of Education
    Publications
Kristina Leeb-Lundberg, Chapter 4
Melanie Rose White, Chapter 8: p. 170

Library of Congress Catalog Card Number: 84-60160
ISBN Catalog Number: 0-912674-86-5
NAEYC #132

Printed in the United States of America

Contents

Preface

As a young teacher, I once met an acquaintance I had not seen in years.

"What do you do?" she asked.

"I teach."

"What do you teach?"

"Nursery school."

The lady looked a little puzzled.

"*What* do you teach in nursery school?"

I must admit that I had no ready answer. Seeing my embarrassment, she quickly provided a reply for me,

"Oh, I know, *nursery rhymes!*"

It probably would have been less awkward for me had I answered, "I help children learn." But even here the stumbling block comes with the next question: "Learn *what?*"

This book attempts to provide a partial answer: mathematics, science, social studies—respectable disciplines, as they are furthered through block building.

The full truth, however, lies elsewhere. The disciplines as we know them are arbitrary divisions of human understanding. Certainly, young children gain experiential foundations that enable them to build understandings of a verbal, abstract nature in later years. Certainly, teachers must know and *must know how to tell others* that these activities are vital and why this is so. Let us not put the cart before the horse, however. What we provide with blocks is experience with a material, combining structure and freedom in a felicitous way.

The pure geometrical forms of unit blocks remind us of Edna St. Vincent Millay's lines:

"Euclid alone has looked on bare beauty."

The pleasure of blocks stems primarily from the aesthetic experience. It involves the whole person—muscles and senses, intellect and emotion, individual growth and social interaction. Learning results from the imaginative activity, from the need to pose and solve problems. True learning occurs, according to Duncker, when disparate thoughts suddenly jell and the individual says "Aha!"

Or as Piaget formulated it, cognitive growth occurs through physical maturation coupled with firsthand experience.

Blocks further these processes.

This volume examines *some* of these aspects in detail. We can never encompass the whole.

Elisabeth S. Hirsch

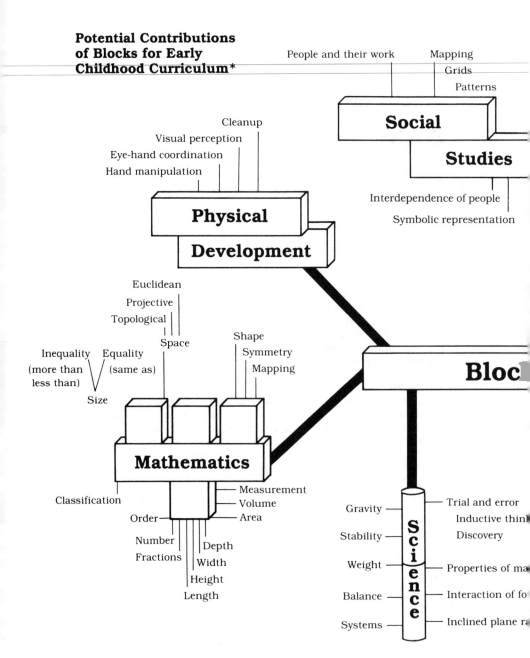

Potential Contributions of Blocks for Early Childhood Curriculum*

People and their work

Mapping
Grids
Patterns

Social

Studies

Interdependence of people

Symbolic representation

Cleanup
Visual perception
Eye-hand coordination
Hand manipulation

Physical

Development

Euclidean
Projective
Topological
Space

Shape
Symmetry
Mapping

Bloc

Inequality
(more than
less than)

Equality
(same as)

Size

Mathematics

Classification

Measurement
Volume
Area

Order

Number
Fractions

Depth
Width
Height

Length

Gravity
Stability
Weight
Balance
Systems

Science

Trial and error
Inductive thin
Discovery

Properties of ma

Interaction of fo

Inclined plane ra

*Adapted from Charlotte and Milton Brody.
The Block Book, edited by Elisabeth S. Hirsch
National Association for the Education of Young Children
1834 Connecticut Avenue, N.W.
Washington, D.C. 20009

viii

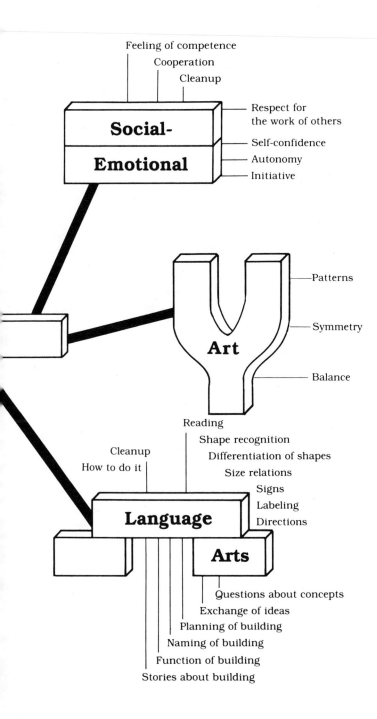

Feeling of competence
Cooperation
Cleanup

Social-Emotional

Respect for the work of others
Self-confidence
Autonomy
Initiative

Art

Patterns
Symmetry
Balance

Reading
Shape recognition
Differentiation of shapes
Size relations
Signs
Labeling
Directions

Cleanup
How to do it

Language Arts

Questions about concepts
Exchange of ideas
Planning of building
Naming of building
Function of building
Stories about building

Introduction

The revised edition of *The Block Book* brings a new format, some additional pictures, and an important new chapter by Elizabeth Dreier.

Like the mother of many children, who always seems to love best the child at whom she happens to be looking, we devoted all our love and attention to unit blocks. We disregarded other size-related unstructured building materials such as hollow blocks and various table blocks.

These neglected siblings share strong family characteristics with our unit blocks. Many of the generalizations discussed in the following chapters apply to them as well. They also have individual characteristics, however.

Hollow wooden blocks, for instance, elicit wonderful dramatic play. They allow children to put themselves into the structure and thus become people who live in the house, own the store, sail the ship, drive the car, or whatever else they wish to understand better through acting it out. Most schools reserve hollow blocks for outdoor use, but there is no reason why they cannot be used indoors, provided there is enough room for building and storage of a sufficient quantity of blocks. Teachers who are able to allow indoor hollow block buildings to remain standing report remarkable projects that not only increase children's understanding of the world, but also enhance group relations and group cohesiveness. Hollow blocks, in addition, are especially suitable for very young children since they involve the use of their large muscles only.

Blocks requiring small-muscle activity, such as Lego, Cuisenaire rods, Geoblocks, Logic-Attribute, or Property-Blocks, have also been disregarded almost completely in this volume. Yet, their advantages are many. Like their bigger brothers and sisters, their use is not prestructured, and their sizes are interrelated. They further the conceptualization of various mathematical and geometrical relationships. These materials become increasingly important as children enter the primary grades.

Piaget's insights about concept formation teach us that intelligence stems from action and that thinking through ideas without the use of manipulative materials is not entirely possible until the end of the elementary school years. As the influence of Piaget and others who apply his ideas reaches wider and wider circles, manufacturers are beginning to supply a growing market with a great variety of table blocks. This is certainly a desirable development. Table blocks will often be sought out by children who wish to do interesting work by themselves.

The underlying conviction shared by all authors in this book pertains to unit blocks, hollow blocks, table blocks, and, indeed, to all other adaptable materials that are part of a rich and stimulating classroom environment.

This conviction, based on a view of how children learn, is summarized masterfully by Charlotte Winsor. A pioneer and a powerful influence in early childhood education, she shares with us her firsthand knowledge of Caroline Pratt, the originator of unit blocks.

The aesthetic experience derived from the activities with blocks was sensitively described by Harriet M. Johnson in her booklet *The Art of Block Building.* This booklet, with its introduction by Lucy Sprague Mitchell, is one of the classics of early childhood literature. It is reprinted here in an abbreviated form.

The scientific concepts that are acquired through firsthand experience with unit blocks are focused on by Mary W. Moffitt. Generalizations about balance, gravity, and space are understood long before their names enter the child's vocabulary. Even more importantly, block building furthers the growth of scientific thinking about inquiry, invention, and discovery.

The chapter "The Block Builder Mathematician" by Kristina Leeb-Lundberg can be read on several levels. It is an introduction to mathematical approaches that many teachers have not encountered before. The author does not expect the early childhood practitioner to become a mathematician, of course, but she feels that an appreciation of the significance of early exploration with blocks will help teachers to value children's spontaneous play with structured materials.

In the chapter "Social Studies and Self-Awareness," Charlotte Brody follows children's interactions with blocks from the first tentative beginnings to the relative sophistication of the primary school age child, who still needs concrete materials for thinking about and understanding social studies concepts. It is interesting to note that Brody and Leeb-Lundberg cite an identical incident to make an entirely different point. The implications of block play are multifaceted.

Harriet K. Cuffaro's thoughts on blocks as a medium for dramatic play are based on many years of living with children and observing their activities. Her perceptiveness and appreciation of children's thinking is evident not only in her own words but also in the charming anecdotes that illuminate her text. Cuffaro's chapter serves as a reminder of the way fantasy play and reality experience overlap in young children's thinking.

The response to the original *Block Book*, first presented ten years ago, was so gratifying that we did not want to change any of the original chapters. However, as teachers become more familiar with Piaget's theories they realize that elementary school children, who still use a concrete operational mode of thinking, will be able to solve problems more effectively if they can use concrete materials. Elizabeth Dreier's chapter illuminates this process through lucid discussion of theory and revealing examples of practice. It is our hope that this addition will help teachers to enrich the learning of school age children in the same way as it was instrumental in encouraging wider use of block building in preschool.

My own convictions about the importance of block play led me to assemble and edit this volume and to write the chapter addressing the nitty-gritty problems of classroom life. This last chapter on how to do it is, however, just one teacher's description of how she did it. Others will have to develop their own style and their own solutions. In this endeavor, the more theoretical considerations of the foregoing chapters should be of inestimable help.

Elisabeth S. Hirsch
New York
January 5, 1984

Charlotte B. Winsor

1

Blocks as a material for learning through play

The contribution of Caroline Pratt

Through the years, there has been much elaboration and interpretation of blocks as a material and block play as a learning method in early childhood education. Since Caroline Pratt's work has long been associated with the development of the basic unit blocks, I have found it useful to seek out her early writings (Pratt 1924; 1948; 1973) and, together with personal recall, attempt to share her thinking about the role of this material in children's learning.

Caroline Pratt was born in 1867 in Fayetteville, a small town in upper New York state. Her childhood and growing years are so much a prototype of rural society in 19th century America and so much written about in story and statistic that they hardly need much further development here. Her lifetime spanned a bursting technology of such magnitude that she recalls, "I remember the day we all went down to the store to see my mother make our first call on the telephone. . . ." And before she was old, Lucy Sprague Mitchell would write

" . . . Modern children are born into an appallingly complicated world. A three-year-old in a city environment may be whisked to his steamheated nursery in an electric elevator, fed from supplies which are ordered by telephone, sent up in a dumb-waiter, and stored in an electric re-

5

frigerator; he may be taken to a hole in the sidewalk and borne rapidly on an underground train to a distant place. The forces which move his elevator, warm his nursery, extend his mother's voice to a grocery store, cool his milk, propel the subway train, are complicated and difficult to understand not only at three, at six, at nine, but even at forty" (Mitchell 1971, p. 12).

And this before the advent of the atomic era, TV, and computers! It is hardly to be wondered then that thoughtful people, then as now, were reassessing the role of the school or that Miss Pratt, with others, was seeking an environment in which children could find appropriate experiences beyond the simple routines of learning to read, write, and reckon.

Similarly, the making of a teacher (teacher education as a professional enterprise was in an embryonic stage at the time) has been expressed tersely, "I pinned up my braids, and there I was—a teacher." For Miss Pratt, it was her great-uncle Homer who said, "Carrie was always good with children," and so, at 16 she became the one teacher in a one-room school in a nearby town. In her words, "I next taught first grade in our village school, and when the children and I were thoroughly weary of the 3R's, I varied the program by teaching the little boys to tip their hats to a woman (Pratt 1948, p. xii). Her teaching style, primitive as it must have been, aroused sufficient interest in the community to get her an offer of a scholarship to Teacher's College in New York.

There she went to begin a lifelong rebellion with traditional methods in education and to search for the meanings in learning that led eventually to the field of childhood education. She was not a happy student, nor a shining light in the courses in kindergarten education to which she was exposed, sensing as she did that much of the content and method of the program might keep the teacher happy, but was hardly of service to the young child's growth needs or capacities. So she turned to manual training, a favorite innovation in education of the 1890s. But again, she found an emptiness of childhood purpose in the exercises she had to master in order that she might pass them on to the children she would teach.

Her first formal teaching assignment, however, was in the manual training shop in a Normal School, where, as she put it, she was "teaching young women to saw to a line." Obviously, she found this nonproductive in her quest and turned to further exploration. In Sweden at this time, there had been developed a school of manual training that moved from performing exercises to making models, and here Miss Pratt went to study at the Sloyd School, only to return with her models, useless to her and certainly meaningless to children.

But she was also studying, reaching out for guidance in new ways of teaching, and attempting the most difficult of all tasks—to formulate an original concept of education " . . . an exploration into the world of children and their ways of growing and learning." It was in these years also that broader concepts of education began to take shape. Social consciousness, aroused by contact with workers and radicals of many schools of thought, became another thread in the pattern of her thinking. Education as a lifelong undertaking for the individual and a force in molding a better world took shape for her.

It was at the turn of the century that Miss Pratt came to live and work in New York City. Here in settlement houses and in one small school, she began to teach real children and to apply some of the principles which had been gestating for some years. She was already convinced that in the process of children's play was the germ of serious learning, indeed a major rehearsal for the tasks awaiting them in growing up.

But such a concept of learning and teaching called for, among other things, the *materials* with which to play. The components of play settings were needed in which children's amorphous ideas could be formulated, dramatized, and perhaps later become accurate statements of reality. Miss Pratt, building on her skills in woodworking, undertook a toy making enterprise, expecting in her naive exuberance to revolutionize education by this backdoor entrance. Her efforts came to nothing at the time, but an approach to early childhood experience through the medium of play materials—toys—remained a basic element of her work.

A first opportunity to try out her ideas and such toys was simply a bare space in a settlement house, where she was permitted a two-month period for her experiment. She volunteered to provide the materials, find the children, and develop a program. To provide the obvious kindergarten materials was a

Blocks would remain simply pieces of wood unless infused with information which is gleaned from experience.

simple task. She was seeking something more—the where-withal with which children could recreate their experiences. She had seen and admired the Patty Hill blocks in the kinder-garten at Teacher's College. But she was seeking a material more flexible and adaptable, that would afford a base line for teaching and learning. She was searching for a truly serious approach to children's play, more than simple playing with blocks in free time. She believed that teachers could provide richer content for play through the experiences they offered children.

It was for this settlement house experiment that Miss Pratt planned what was to become her design for an early childhood classroom. In her words " . . . There were the blocks I had made, and the toys I designed and made myself; there were the crayons and papers and there was clay . . . I had made it as easy and inviting as I knew how, and then I stood aside and let them forage for themselves." One of the six five-year-olds whom she had recruited for her program put her theory about childhood play into practice. "I couldn't have asked for a more appropriate demonstration of my belief in the serious value of children's play. Michael was so deeply absorbed . . . he might have been a scientist working out an experiment in a laboratory. . . . With blocks to help him, he was using all his mental powers, reasoning out relationships . . . and drawing conclusions. He was learning to think" (Pratt 1948, pp. 31–32).

The results of this brief experiment would have been frustrating, as well as exhilarating, had it not been for an offer of further support for her work. Once more, Miss Pratt found a few five-year-olds whose parents were ready to let her play school with them. Her name for this undertaking was indeed the Play School, but with vastly deeper meanings for her.

Her emphasis from here onward seemed to turn toward the development of a body of content which children could build upon in their play. Their idiosyncratic expression of experience was valued, at least theoretically. For one child, a trip to the docks—a much used learning center in this little school—might be expressed in blocks as a rather accurate representation of an ocean liner; while for another, a large expanse of blue paint on paper might recreate the experience of the vast river. But, basically, to build knowledge about the world in which one lives, and with the autonomy and the tools (materials, among which blocks held high priority) with which to express such knowledge, was at the crux of this method.

It is interesting to note that nowhere in Miss Pratt's writings is there a specific reference to the invention of the unit blocks which came to be associated with her name. In fact, many years later, when her beloved City and Country School was in dire financial straits, and it was suggested that the blocks be patented, she resisted angrily, insisting that blocks would remain simply pieces of wood unless infused with a body of information which is gleaned from experience.

Writing some years later in a description of the Play School, she offers her premise, "Toys and blocks do not respond to the need of a child who has no related knowledge to fall back upon. If a child does not know that a horse's home is a stable, where he is fed and cared for, if he does not know the use either of a horse or a wagon, it is useless to present him with a horse and wagon to play with" (Winsor 1973, p. 28). Such experience for the New York City child may seem quaint today, but her principle of play as learning experience is stated explicitly. One must also infer the active role of the adult in providing experience appropriate to age level needs and the furthering of primary experience by discussion, materials, and analysis, if one may use the term.

And in this statement is embodied, more than blocks as a material for play, a philosophy of learning with play as its springboard. Miss Pratt believed that children perceive their need for enriched information, not per se, not to gratify the adult's wish to teach them, but in order to enhance the quality of their play. They raise new inquiries which carry on to the discovery of further intellectual relationships. An example may be in order here. Children build boats, especially in a seaport city. In an early stage of the child's development, some essential physical characteristics are presented, the shape of the boat, the sounds it makes. But then the questions come. *Where does it go? How do people get to land?* Then, *what is a dock? Further, what is the boat carrying? Who makes it go?* And, still later, *what are the essentials of transportation in the real world?* The sensitive skill of the teacher is called upon to nurture appropriate questions and answers with the children and, most important, to provide experience within which children may find answers for themselves. And the new knowledge pays its own dividend, namely, more fun in their play world. One may hypothesize that by such methods, children find the very quest for knowledge a gratifying experience, and the learning process moves.

The implementation in depth of much of Miss Pratt's theoretical stance became possible with the founding and growth of the City and Country School. Together with Harriet Johnson and Lucy Sprague Mitchell, she was able to recruit numbers of children, observe them in the hands of specially prepared teachers over long periods of time (from infancy to adolescence), and record behavior in group and individual experiences. Miss Johnson's formulation, arrived at from exhaustive recording and study of very young children's use of blocks, offers three major points of emphasis: first, " . . . the power to deal effectively with his environment accrues to a child through the free use of constructive material;" second, " . . . possibilities are offered by blocks and similar materials for expressing rhythm, pattern, design;" and, third, " . . . by means of these materials, children may review, rehearse and play out their past experience" (Johnson 1972, pp. 183, 189).

In these deceptively simple statements, one finds a structure which encompasses the major principles of child growth. What is meant by that first statement and where does its import take us? Children's strength lies in their vigorous need for action, leading on to a grasping for competence. This they can best achieve by mastery of appropriate materials. Miss Pratt carries such thinking further in stating one of her fervent beliefs, "The unfortunate child is the one who has his interest riveted in people, because he cannot manage them, convert them to his purposes. They dominate him and he is converted to their purposes" (Pratt 1924, p. 5).

The second statement tells us that such materials serve, by their very freedom, more than the realistic purpose of recreating the known. The young child who laid down blocks rhythmically, decorated the structure fancifully, and named it "just a sign," tells us that these seemingly plain materials can become a veritable artist's palette for some children.

The third statement comes very close to a definition of play offered many years later by Erikson, who proposes a theory, "That the child's play is the infantile form of human ability to deal with experience by creating model situations and to master reality by experimenting and planning" (1950, p. 195).

In many schools, blocks are a basic material for the older children in the nursery years. For them, there develop more elaborate expectations, a further intellectual (academic) exploitation of the possible learnings. As has been indicated earlier, the content of children's play—information about reality— was viewed as an essential ingredient when such play is seen as having a major role in the learning process. The facts of our world and its workings become the scripts for the dramas played out in block schemes, as they are called. Such a scheme demands preplanning, group organization with specialization of tasks, buildings sufficiently true to reality to serve as settings and sturdily engineered to withstand real play.

For this author, remembrances of such block schemes fill the mind. One such experience may be worth a description. Upon a return from a trip to a nearby building site, one child drew a primitive floor plan on a large piece of paper. Dramatically, he unrolled this before his companions and directed them to their various building jobs. Only then did the teacher recall seeing the supervisor on the job using a blueprint with the workers. And it should be added this was only the beginning of a play scheme which lasted several days and was elaborated as the children built the structure, dramatized the functions of the builders, and finally drew into their play other children to be tenants of their building.

The opportunity for social studies content arising from such block play boggles the mind and needs to be used judiciously, lest one forget the axiom of readiness for receiving stimuli. And one could make as good a case for math or science or reading. But others will undertake to discuss these aspects of blocks as a material in early childhood programs.

Another question, much pondered, is what supplementary materials best serve block play? Here Caroline Pratt was, at least to this author, an absolute purist. No reason to provide a car, an animal, or a truck when the child could improvise or make a crude replica of a needed object, said she. In fact, one deep virtue for her in this material was the way it led children to creativity with other materials—e.g., wood to fashion a car, clay to model a figure, paints or crayon to indicate a needed river or street. Supplementary materials therefore should be adaptable to a variety of uses—cloth, bits of wire, or hose, or oddly shaped pieces of wood, the springs of an old clock, or whatever the ingenuity of the teacher brought to the class to stimulate the imagination toward an original solution of a problem in the children's constructions. The settings she valued were austere to the point of barrenness, yet, somehow, presenting children with a clarity of choice and becoming with time real workshops for children. How sharply such settings contrast with many of our nursery classrooms today, often filled with commercial products so finished as to dictate their use with little adaptablity to the child's imaginative purposes.

Perhaps, inevitably, children, as all of us, are living in a world further than ever removed from the primary processes of their

Blocks offer an almost infinite variety of expressive opportunity from designs to veritable engineering feats of bridge building. But blocks remain a means rather than an end in the learning process.

existence. Whether the school can or should attempt to bring to the child opportunities for unraveling some of our complexities is a baffling imponderable.

Only faith in the children themselves and the prime importance of play as their mode of experimentation and discovery can offer a base for further exploration of the true value of the materials in the programs of early childhood education.

One may summarize the body of principles that have governed this approach to childhood learning in the following statements:

■ The child needs an autonomous and active role in the learning process.

■ Play is the process by which the child's experience is expressed and organized.

■ Play is enriched as further experience including primary and vicarious information becomes available.

■ Development of play requires adaptable materials which can serve fantasy as well as reality experience.

■ Blocks offer an almost infinite variety of expressive opportunity from floor patterns or designs to veritable engineering feats of bridge building. But blocks remain a means rather than an end in the learning process.

■ Children can achieve true mastery of adaptable materials in their own terms and know the gratification of competence at their level of maturity without dependence upon adult judgment of a given product.

■ The teaching role becomes complementary to the process—providing, enriching, leading on to further experience.

■ Beyond any material lies the need for adult understanding of the child's maturity level and growth, which becomes the base line upon which materials and experience are provided.

References

Erikson, E. H. *Childhood and Society.* New York: Norton, 1950.

Johnson, H. *Children in the Nursery School.* New York: Agathon Press, 1972. Reissued with an introductory essay by Barbara Biber.

Mitchell, L. S. *Young Geographers.* New York: Agathon Press, 1971. Original version 1921.

Pratt, C., ed. *Experimental Practice in the City and Country School.* New York: E. P. Dutton, 1924.

Pratt, C. *I Learn from Children.* New York: Simon and Schuster, 1948.

Pratt, C. "The Play School." In *Experimental Schools Revisited,* ed. C. Winsor. New York: Agathon Press, 1973.

Winsor, C., ed. *Experimental Schools Revisited.* New York: Agathon Press, 1973.

Harriet M. Johnson

2

The art of block building

Introduction

What are blocks for?

Toy makers have put blocks on the market for many long years, decorating them with letters of the alphabet in an attempt to sneak something "useful" into a child's play. But young children usually ignored the letters and piled the blocks into gay towers. Then, some 30 or more years ago, school people began to take children's play seriously, to say that play itself was educational, and a different kind of blocks came on the market. They were just pieces of unpainted wood, the same width and thickness, and with lengths twice or four times as great as the unit block. A few curves, cylinders, and half-thickness blocks were added, but all with lengths that fitted into the measurements of the basic blocks. These blocks, devised by Caroline Pratt, founder of the City and Country School, were in use in the nursery, now called Harriet Johnson Nursery School, which Harriet Johnson directed from its organization in 1914 until her death.

Many schools for young children now use these blocks. They have been found to be the most useful tool for self-education that young children can play with and work with. Most teachers have concentrated on the value of these blocks as giving

This chapter is based on Bank Street College of Education Publications' 1966 reprint of *The Art of Block Building* by Harriet Johnson, originally published in 1933.

children an opportunity to reproduce their experiences quickly and then play them out actively with their block creations. Harriet Johnson was well aware of this value and has written about the use of blocks in *Children in the Nursery School* (1972).

In the present study, however, Harriet Johnson has concentrated on another value of the blocks, a value often overlooked. These blocks in the creative hands of children also become an art medium. Grown-ups are still prone to organize a curriculum for one "area of learning" and then another, and to work out equipment which they think will develop one patch of a child and then another. But children just refuse to respond in this piecemeal fashion. They remain consistently whole people, reacting to situations with all their lively interests mixed together. They are small scientists eagerly investigating the world that they can lay their hands on; small human beings interested in other human beings; dramatists playing out their experiences, modifying them to give themselves a strategic position in the world of grown-ups; workmen exulting in their techniques; artists enjoying design and pattern-form, balance in size and color, repetition. The wonder of blocks is the many-sided constructive experiences they yield to the many-sided constructive child—and every child is such if guided by a many-sided constructive parent or teacher.

Harriet Johnson was such a teacher. She watched the young children in her nursery school with a scientist's eye and recorded with a scientist's accuracy. She appreciated keenly the beauty of these children's creations, as well as the thinking and social interactions and workmanship they involved. Thus she came to write *The Art of Block Building* (1933). Here she has separated from the many-sided experiences children live through in their block building the elusive element that we call "art," a precious element seldom lacking in children's work, but, alas, seldom recognized by teachers or parents whose eyes are so earnestly fixed on "bringing up a child right" that they fail to enjoy children and their art.

Lucy Sprague Mitchell
April 1945

* * *

In the school of which I am writing, (which was called the Nursery School of the Bureau of Education Experiments, later called the Harriet Johnson Nursery School, and now named Bank Street School for Children) and in others with which I am familiar, block building is one of the major interests. A description of the activities of these schools or a discussion of their curricula would show constructive play with blocks as a central and coordinating feature of their programs.

As I have watched block building over a period of years, the method by which children develop techniques in construction and the versatility they show in their use of blocks have been of increasing interest to me. Still more absorbing has been the realization that almost inevitably, in the block building history of group after group, there appear art forms, comparable in spirit to those produced by older children with plastic materials such as paints or clay.

I have tried to present in these pages the use of blocks as a medium of expression and to give a glimpse of the ideas and feelings expressed by children from two to six years of age.

The first use of blocks among young children is not properly building. Blocks are carried from place to place, or they may be stacked or massed in irregular, conglomerate piles before the period of construction begins. During this time, children probably are probably getting an experience no less real than their later one when adults can recognize the result as illustrating actual problems in balance, construction, design, or representation. The early experience holds value because of the chance to gain acquaintance with this particular building tool by manipulation and by using various forms and various spaces.

Between two and three years of age, real construction begins and has been found to follow broadly three or four lines of development, especially in regard to the techniques. Blocks in these early years are comparable to such plastic materials as crayons, paint, or clay, and their use is dependent upon impulse, which is influencing the young builder.

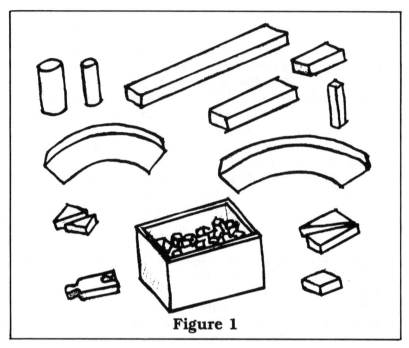

Figure 1

**The blocks and accessories in the set above were those used at Bank
Street by Harriet Johnson. Sets vary in types of blocks and accessories, depending on the manufacturer, but all blocks are based on the
following proportions—1:2:4 (half as high are they are wide; twice
as long as they are wide).**

The blocks in use in the indoor playrooms are shown here
(Figure 1). These blocks were designed by Caroline Pratt and
have always been used in the City and Country School. She has
never given them her name and so they are found on the market under the name of the manufacturer and under various
trade names. It will be seen that all the other forms can be
made from the unit by multiplication or division, except the
cylinders or curves. The cylinders conform in height to the unit
and posts. The curves are of similar width and thickness. In
addition to the other forms, small colored cubes one-inch
square are used.

It is essential that the blocks be cut very accurately so that all
edges are even and that the multiples and divisions of the unit

are exact, because they are tools for the children's use, and the most desirable building habits will be established only if the materials are stable and precise.

Occasionally the illustrations show blocks other than those in the set described above. This occurs only in the youngest groups where a wider variety of materials is provided.

The sketches of actual constructions made by the children are taken from the daily records of teachers and students. They are accurate in the kind and number of blocks used, but because they were made hastily and because few of us are skilled in drafting, they are far from accurate in perspective and proportion. They are not drawn to the same scale, because they were designed only as a graphic record of the day's building activity.

Repetition, the tower, and the row

All parents and teachers will agree that repetition in one form or another is characteristic of children who are just beginning to perfect their locomotion or their language. They climb up steps only to descend and climb again. They throw a ball only to retrieve it and throw again, unless they can induce an adult to take one step in the repetitive process. After they learn to say "I slide down" or "Want see," adults turn gray as the refrain beats on their tired ears.

It has been very interesting to us to find repetition in many forms appearing again and again as the first constructive use of blocks.

A child can repeat by piling blocks one on top of another. At first, the resulting tower may be an irregular one, threatening to fall as each additional block is placed. At this stage, lofty towers are not found in the records, because they crash before a sketch can be made of them.

Early differences in personality traits are plainly shown here. There are children who, from the first, attempt to straighten their block edges and who do not try for perilous heights, seemingly able to judge when the last steady block is in place. There are others who fling their blocks together, not concerned with the perfection or the stability of the structure.

Whichever method individual children choose, the general tendency toward repetition is universal. Among the youngest children, it almost seems as if their object is to clear all shelves, so persistently do they add another and another and another block to a tower or a row, or as will be seen, repeat a pattern over and over again.

Edith, who had discovered that blocks were not just luggage but building material, achieved this tower—first one block and then another, laid as nearly as possible in the same place (Figure 2).

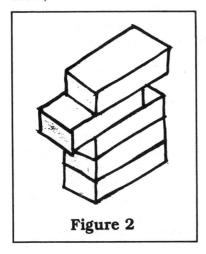

Figure 2

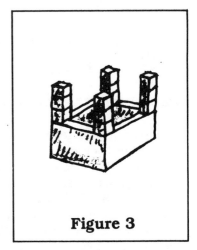

Figure 3

None of the methods in use among young builders is superseded entirely by new and elaborate building techniques. Rather each form evolves into more and more detailed constructions, which are more and more difficult to execute as skill of hand and an understanding of the possibilities within the material develop.

At first the evolution takes the form of experimenting within the chosen plan. Having made a pile of blocks, perhaps all of one kind, builders vary the kind or combine kinds or they do stunt building, balancing large blocks on a smaller base or on a narrow support.

Danny placed a tower of three cubes on each corner of his cube box (Figure 3). This was a task requiring care and delicacy

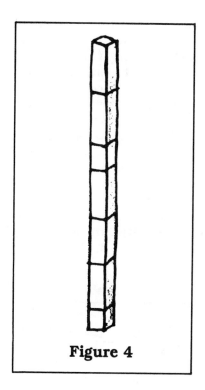

Figure 4

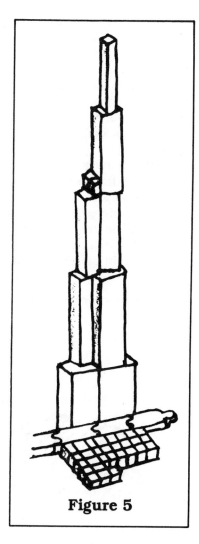

Figure 5

of handling as he began on the nearer corners and reached across the first towers to place blocks on the further ones.

Sasha tried repeating balancing stunts with units and half units (Figure 4). While placing the two top blocks, she steadied those below with her left hand.

Henry took blocks of various sizes to make his tower (Figure 5). The trains and the flooring of cubes seemed to be accessories.

With the data on hand, it is impossible to tell whether or not the tower is an earlier pattern than the row. Traditional influences, as well as modern tendencies, are at work toward establishing an interest in height. Also, to lay one block upon another may be a simpler process than to place one next to another in a line. The examples given here of the tower and the row were made within the same month. The recipe is similar: first one block and then another is placed in serial order on the floor.

Later, when less hampered by the difficulties of mere manipulation of the material, children embroider the pattern in a variety of ways. Instead of laying the blocks closely side by side or edge to edge, they may space them, alternating the sizes as they place them or alternating single blocks with low tiers.

Repetition follows a syncopated rhythm in Danny and Henry's building (Figures 6, 7, 8, 9).

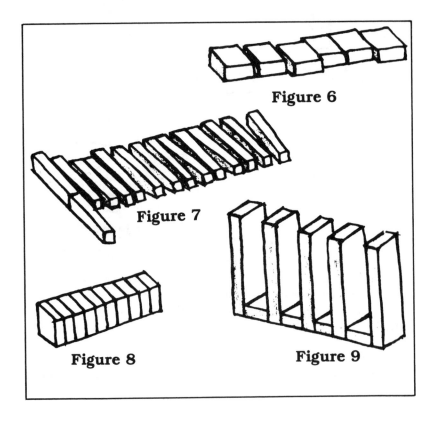

Figure 6

Figure 7

Figure 8

Figure 9

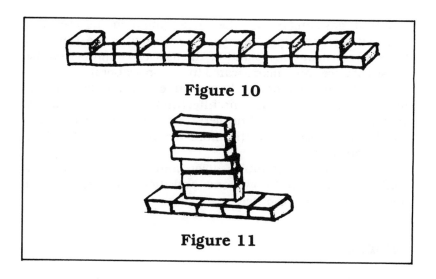

Figure 10

Figure 11

These two patterns (Figures 10, 11), the tower and the row, are preeminently characteristic of youthful building. Sometimes, towers and rows are combined.

When children can make single towers with blocks on edge as well as flat on their faces or with combinations of sizes or shapes, they find that a series of towers makes a wall, just as a series of rows makes a floor (Figure 12).

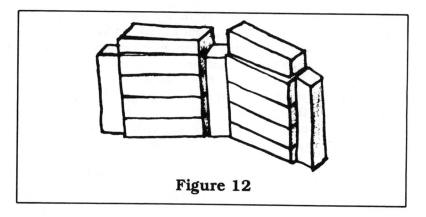

Figure 12

At first, handling blocks, then arranging them in towers and rows, or walls and flooring, absorbs children. Interest in these types of construction in and of themselves is short lived, because they are soon incorporated into more elaborate constructions. They are no longer valued as an end, but only as a technique and a detail in larger architectural planning. It is almost as if the first year of building were a practice period which is to lay the foundations for the more technical work of the advanced student.

Beneath all the examples given and illustrated runs the youthful pattern: put down one, and then another, and then another, and then another.

Bridging

After a time given these architecurally exact building materials, certain problems in construction invariably seem to arise. By this I mean that although no patterns are set and no suggestions are made by the teachers, the constructions made increase in elaboration and in difficulty, and fairly predictable stages in the building activities can be observed.

One of the early problems is that of bridging, of setting up two blocks, leaving a space between them and roofing that space with another block.

It is sometimes a difficult problem to place the uprights at an appropriate distance apart, so that the third block will bridge the space. An acute dilemma occurs when one of the longest blocks on the shelves is laid flat, and another is placed upright at each end of it. Such a problem has been known to block some children completely, and the younger child is usually defeated at the first failure.

Edith twice set up the figure sketched, all three blocks double units, and tried to bridge the space with a double (Figure 13).

She then set up a, b, and c (doubles) and tried to bridge them as usual with another double. When she found that it would not fit, she tried it across c (dotted lines), then laid it in position x, and added y (Figure 14).

Danny spaced four double units on end, but did no more about it (Figure 15).

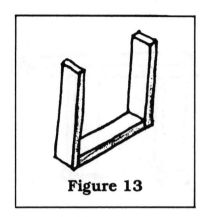

Figure 13

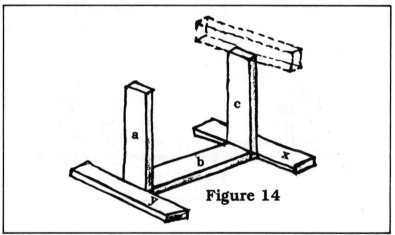

Figure 14

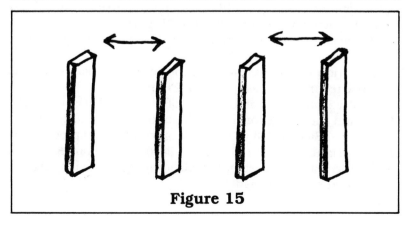

Figure 15

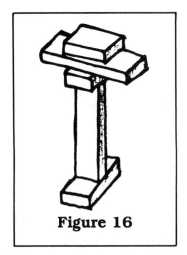

Figure 16

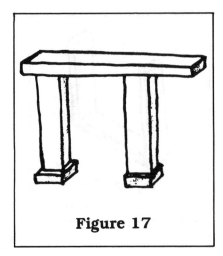

Figure 17

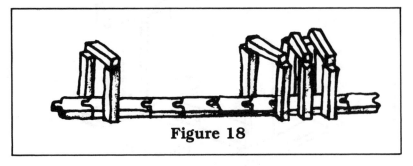

Figure 18

He approached success here, though his bridge did not yet span a space between two uprights (Figure 16).

This was followed by achieving the bridge technique (Figure 17).

Repetition takes possession of the young builder as soon as the new technique is established (Figure 18).

Facility leads to a combination of styles and methods. The tower and the bridge form "a high building" with "fire ladders" at the side. Sasha built as shown (Figure 19), then propped the three uprights against the "high building." She showed elation when the feat was accomplished, jumping and clapping her hands and smiling broadly.

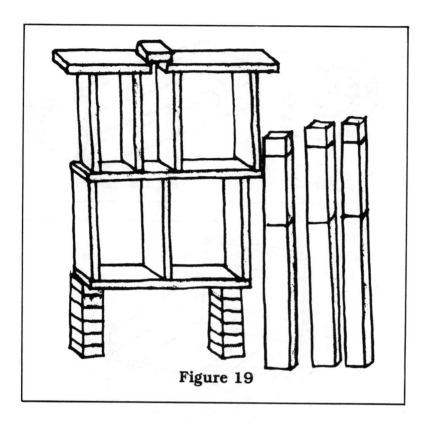

Figure 19

Enclosures

Enclosures appear early in the building activities. To put four blocks together so that a space is completely enclosed is not a simple task. However it appears, and once learned, repetitive enclosures seem to be the next step. That is, every new device, idea, method, or pattern lends itself to the repetitive formula.

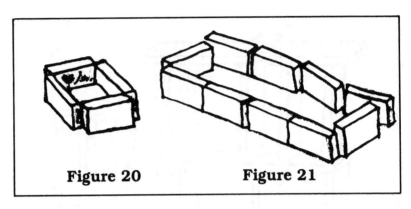

Figure 20   **Figure 21**

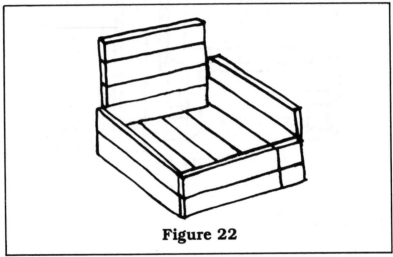

Figure 22

Sarah worked for a full month before she succeeded in placing the last block which completely enclosed a space (Figures 20, 21). The driving force was her own initiative.

Sarah later built double units and two half units as shown (Figure 22)—a marked elaboration of her first attempt.

Fancy free, now that skill of hand had been acquired, Sarah arranged her enclosures in patterned, repetitive form (Figure 23).

Danny arranged a row of four enclosures (Figure 24). Repetition takes the field.

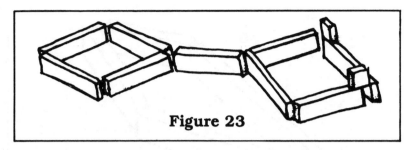

Figure 23

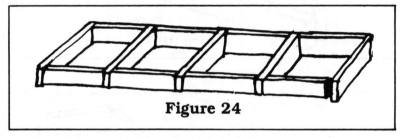

Figure 24

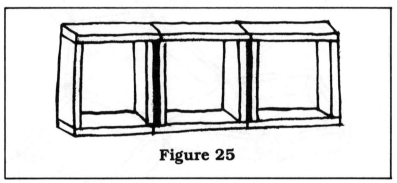

Figure 25

This time, he set his enclosures on end—or are they a series of bridges?—first one, and then another, and then another (Figure 25).

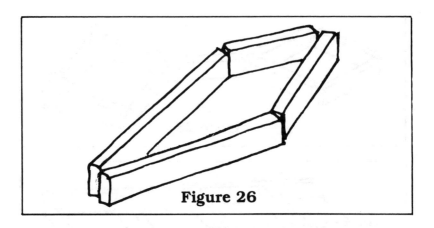

Figure 26

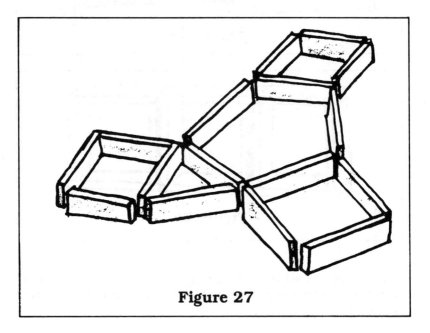

Figure 27

Michael varied the square design (Figure 26).

Here are enclosures repeated and elaborated. Michael set double units on edges, making a most pleasing pattern (Figure 27). He began with the pentagon, then added the triangle. He did not achieve the square and triangle at the first placing of

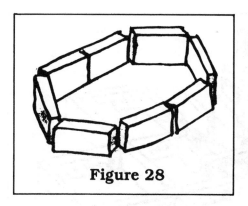

Figure 28

the blocks, but pushed them about. He said, "Pushing them in" once as he worked, but was not heard to name his building.

Let no academic adult here raise the question: "Do you call children's attention to the shapes they have made, the rectangle, the triangle, the pentagon, and give them their names?" The experience which building holds for children is varied, to be sure, but it is useless unless it springs from some impulse within them. At this stage, they are wrestling with the problem of making material (which to the uninformed adult may seem factual and unyielding) take on the quality of plasticity and almost of malleability. It will yield to the child's desire. Children are absorbed, intent, and satisfied during this process, as anyone who has watched a block building period can testify. Information is completely irrelevant here. It would remain irrelevant even if we granted that the subject was one suited to the preschool ages.

Michael, still intent upon odd-shaped enclosures, builds what he calls "the wow wow circle" (Figure 28).

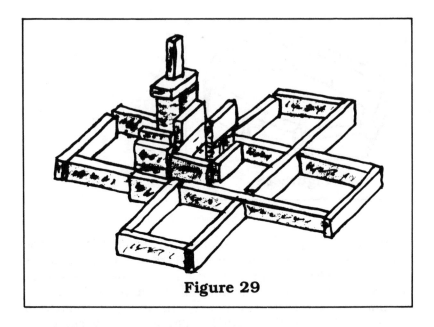

Figure 29

Enclosures become more elaborate. This (Figure 29) was called "a house," and dolls were placed in each section.

When children are once able to see blocks as building material which is capable of being put together in an ordered arrangement, a variety of methods, patterns, and techniques seem to suggest themselves to them. With age, there is a steady increase in facility, imagination, elaboration of design, and actual number of blocks used.

Patterns

As soon as children begin to acquire facility in the use of blocks, so that they feel at home with the material, another tendency appears, namely that of building in balanced and decorative patterns. We have been led to the conclusion that blocks are essentially the most admirable plastic material for young children, because with blocks they seem able to arrange, to design, to compose.

I do not wish to imply that children say, even to themselves,

"Now I will make a design," but that with child after child in a group, with child after child of age after age, unnamed and unused buildings appear, delightful to the adult eye in the rhythm of their balance and the originality of their design and decoration.

In such decorative buildings are incorporated any or all of the building principles described, and with them, the repetitive impulse finds full scope; in fact, repetition is one of the features of design.

Again, it must be said that no patterns are set for the children, that no comments are made upon their buildings except in the way of general response to a given child's explanation or remark. Occasionally, children are asked, "Would you like to build?", or they are told that they may use any kind of block if they seem to be inclined to restrict themselves to one size. In the beginning of the school year, the children are shown the blocks and are told that they may build. The only restriction placed upon the use of the materials is that they are not to be thrown and that structures are not to be knocked down. Probably the most potent factor in establishing a creative use of blocks is the genuine interest of the teachers in block building as an expressive art—an outlet for the manifold experiences through which children are living, whether they are the intentional experiences of the school or those that life itself thrusts upon them. In children's reaction to their "work," the teachers see such evidences of interest, absorption, and elation that their enthusiasm is kindled.

When a child who has not had the experience with block building comes into a group at four or five years of age, that child seems to follow much the same order of development that younger children do, but of course passes through the various phases at a much more rapid rate of speed. The steps or stages that have been described seem invariably to appear first. The rate at which children pass through these stages, the emphasis they place on each, and the lines of development that they subsequently follow vary with their individuals.

The inclination to seek a patterned arrangement also varies, but only, I think, in degree. There are few young builders who seem to lack a feeling for pattern and balance. For the most part, the design they follow is more or less evenly balanced,

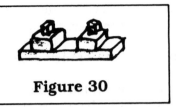

Figure 30

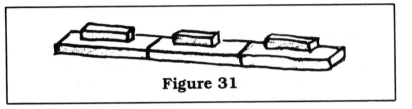

Figure 31

almost a formal one. Often the rhythm is a muscular one; that is, the child places a block at the right, then at the left, or a block at the front of a construction, then at the back. The fact that opposite sides of a large construction are in absolute balance even when the design is intricate, seems to suggest that the builder is dominated by an image, whether kinesthetic or visual, we do not know.

However, younger children, having completed structures which in the opinion of adults are quite perfect, often massed blocks all about and concealed the patterns entirely in conglomerate piles, as if they either did not see the patterns or did not value them.

Just why did Edith choose from the block shelves this varied combination (Figure 30)? Both cubes set on top were yellow.

At the same age, she made this very similar pattern, but here she has taken length for her accent and has placed posts—evenly spaced—on each of the double units (Figure 31).

Danny, still very much in the stage of stacking, made this very unusal arrangement of posts (Figure 32). More were laid than sketched here. In spite of its being a rather tricky pattern to follow consistently, the alteration was maintained.

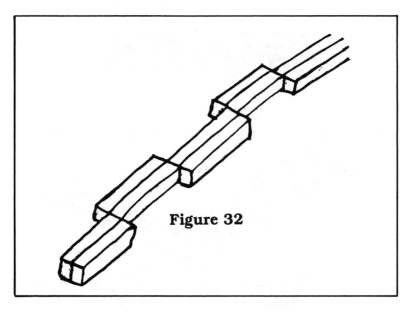

Figure 32

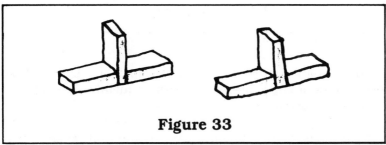

Figure 33

How can a child who has worked so little with this material, who is so immature in other details of development, in language, and indeed in block building, keep consistently in mind this sort of alteration? The answer is probably that he did not keep it in mind but in muscle, or at least that it was feeling, not thinking, that guided him.

Sometimes the pattern is a small one, repeated again and again. Sarah used posts as illustrated (Figure 33).

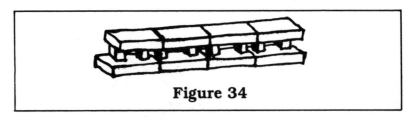

Figure 34

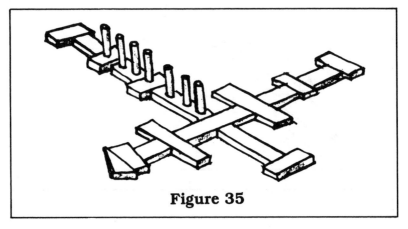

Figure 35

This design (Figure 34) in layers, small cubes tucked between rows of larger blocks, appears frequently. Tony did not name his construction.

Spreading, flat buildings were characteristic of Tony. The conventional balance does not possess him as it seems to possess some children, but to the adult onlooker the design element has charm.

At this age, naming may be a part of building, so this (Figure 35) is a "Big, long, long train."

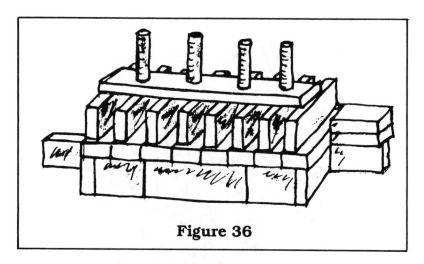

Figure 36

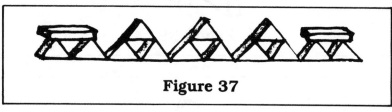

Figure 37

This building (Figure 36) which Tony made four months later was unnamed. It illustrates the way structures become more intricate as children grow older.

One feels a lovely balance in Ingrid's building (Figure 37). She made just this, then left it. She did not name it.

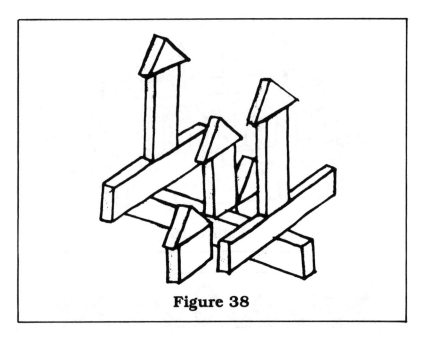

Figure 38

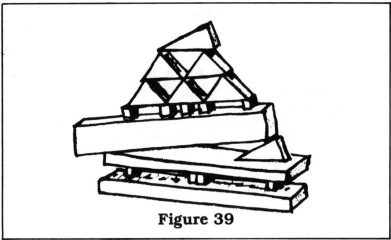

Figure 39

Rather difficult task this was, to balance long blocks on their edges and to place the upright unit with its triangle cap at a point where it can hold the balance (Figure 38).

Judith was a child aware of an intention, for she called this (Figure 39) "decoration."

Representation

Somewhere along in the early block building history, an impulse to name arises. This does not mean that the buildings resemble the things they are called. Children may give names to their constructions, or their drawings, because of the example of older children who do so with intention, or, more probably, because of injudicious adult questioning. Teachers are quite careful to avoid suggesting, even by questions, that children name their buildings, because they have learned that real representative building comes at a later stage.

Among two- and three-year-old children, we find naming, but very rarely play use of the structures made with small indoor blocks. Naming becomes very usual among older children. The name is often announced as an advance plan. Dramatic use of buildings increases as the techniques of building are well learned, so that the material is no longer master of the situation as it is earlier.

At later ages, the dramatic impulse is so strong that the buildings reproduce or symbolize actual structures or experiences which the children are recalling and serve as stage settings. A group of children build a railway system, tracks, stations, switching engines, a tower for the signal attendant and even the building to which the railroad employees go to to get their watches tested. These standpatter (dolls made of copper wire, with lead feet and wooden beads for heads and hands) employees took their meals on a roof garden constructed by one of the girls in the group. All the buildings in this play scheme were built by individuals, but the play with them afterward was cooperative and interrelated. Play of this sort represents a fairly mature understanding.

Other materials, like crayons and clay, are more freely in use and serve as supplements to the play or as elaborations of it. Tools have been introduced so that bench products can be made and added to the scheme of play of which the block building is the center.

With all the opportunities for elaboration of the representative structures, we find some surprising, though probably logical, developments. In the first place, we realize as we look at the block buildings that repetition continues to be much in

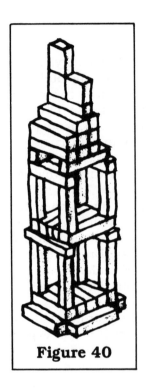

Figure 40

Figure 41

evidence. The tower has grown more complicated, but its construction still means placing first one block and then another in a pile of sorts. The pile may be foursquare, made of repeated bridge units superimposed one upon another, or it may be an enclosure of solid walls. Children call upon all the techniques they acquired in their early experimenting period, combining the simple patterns, including many in a single structure, and using many more blocks in the process. Secondly, with the increasing tendency of children to give names to their structures, we find the design elements persisting and becoming more intricate and, at the same time, taking on attributes which we usually associate with symbolism as we know it in the artistic sense.

Henry's building (Figure 40) strikes a commonly accepted pattern in general movement, the larger base narrowing to the slender, terminal tower, quite in unrecognized acceptance of

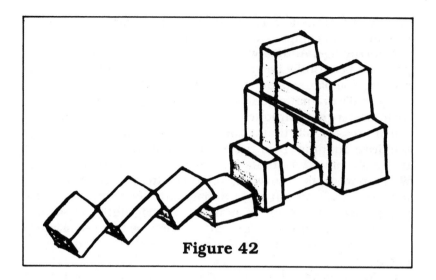

Figure 42

New York's set-back fashion. Henry's name for his tower, "a park," may have meant that he had observed buildings in a park or, more probably, it may have been an overflow from his awakening social and language interest. That he also mentioned bridges, smokestacks, and doors to the entranced Joan (who listened, watched, and tried to direct him) suggests that his language was not closely related to his building. The three small blocks at the tip of the tower were called "lights."

Andrea's "Empire State" is an illustration of a very practical cob house construction with very little elaboration (Figure 41). Its name is almost inevitable, since Manhattan is dominated by that vertiginous piece of architecture.

Betty came through with a statement: "A house and these are the stairs" (Figure 42).

Do children see stairs in some such pattern or are they unable to grasp the technique of making gradually decreasing piles, set side by side? Since they can build a train shed completely enclosed, so that no train can enter or leave it, since they make a high chair for the baby taller than the house in which it is to be placed, since the early drawing of a boat may be a collection of smokestacks and funnels, we know that the young hand needs much practice and that though the young mind can assimilate certain outstanding features, it does not take in a total complicated conception.

At a later age, Andrea was quite capable of using stairs as a part of a beautifully balanced building (Figure 43), and of arranging doll blankets on them as carpets.

The really dramatic quality about these young builders is not their mastery of techniques but their attitude toward the material. It is essentially that of the artist. Even when they do representative building, it is the essence, not the bald form, that they make alive. We adults are prosaic in the use of our skills. We learn to speak or to write, and thereafter practice these arts in a strictly utilitarian and unimaginative fashion. It is a rare person whose speech is marked by originality or whose thoughts find expression in written language that seems really her or his own—that has the quality of the individual producing it.

Children speak with blocks. They say in their own way what they have to say. It may be fanciful or humorous. They may express a resemblance or a parallel in their building, or a symbol may stand for a complex conception.

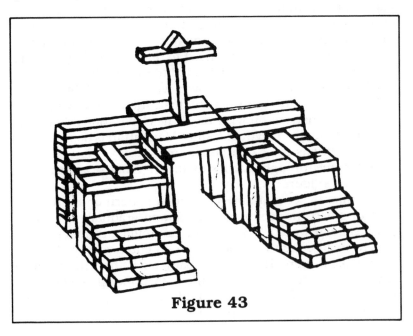

Figure 43

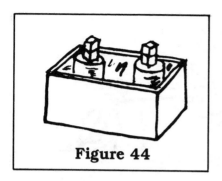

Figure 44

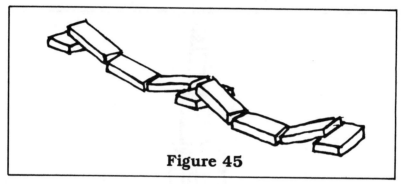

Figure 45

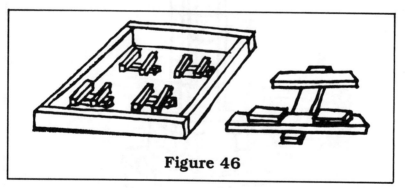

Figure 46

Jeanne sees her two cylinders as "candlesticks," and so do we (Figure 44).

"The river, that goes up and down like waves," was as effective to Jan as an inspired simile to an older poet (Figure 45).

Edward makes a fleet or a litter of "baby airplanes with the mama plane" (Figure 46).

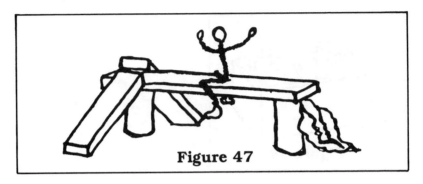

Figure 47

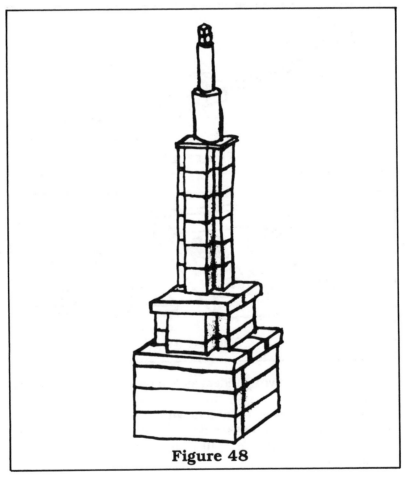

Figure 48

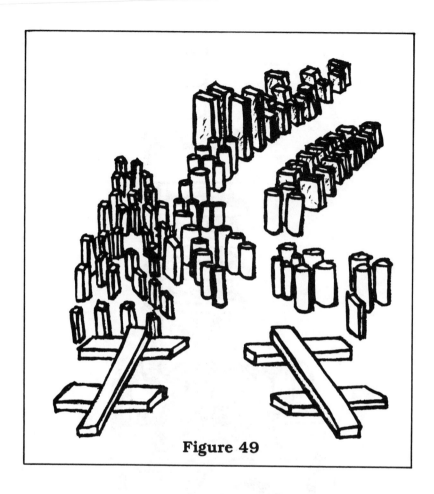

Figure 49

Jackie's "horse with me on it" is an example of how little the limitations of the material need cramp a child (Figure 47).

Richard's "Empire State" is "like the real one, big at the bottom and then smaller" (Figure 48).

John and Lucio saw these blocks, set up on their ends, with imaginative eyes. It is "a parade"—not quite so orderly as some (Figure 49). Perhaps the crowd is gathered to welcome a visiting celebrity. Even the airplanes are here.

Figure 50

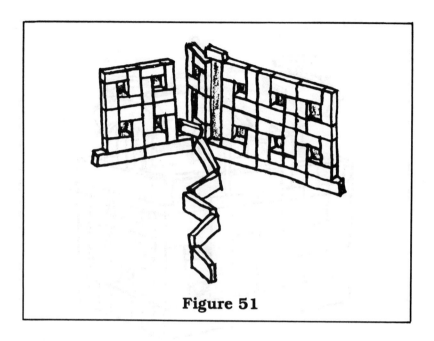

Figure 51

Judith has used a wide variety of material in her unnamed structure (Figure 50). Its balance is not entirely conventional, and therefore perhaps more pleasing to adults.

Norman's "hospital," in its arrangement of planes and lines, has a modern flavor startling to adults (Figure 51). We cannot know what it meant to him—not an experiment in planes, we may be sure, but some sort of an affective experience was his as he worked, absorbed, sober, intent, oblivious of the other builders until the last zigzag block was laid and his work was finished.

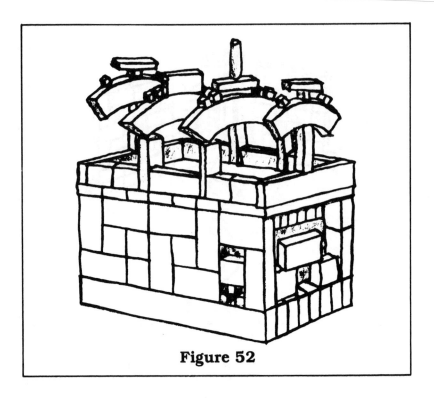

Figure 52

Joel's unnamed structure shows some outstanding features in balance (Figure 52). She has matched the cubes in colors from the right to the left side. She has let in three windows in each of her side walls. Two of them are made after the classic design favored by older builders. In these, the opening will just take a half-unit block. Put in place, it closes the window, as can be seen. The third window on either side has a slightly different construction, making a larger opening. She has apparently raised the sash, holding it up with an arrangement of three cubes. The opposite side of this structure is identical to the one sketched. And so it goes.

The difficulty in gathering these examples from our records has been in deciding which among many to include. Many of the most intricate and enchanting constructions were too elaborate for the lay hand to sketch.

For the most part, I have emphasized what I have called the

use of blocks as art material, rather than their use in dramatic reproduction—the play with form and balance in their use, rather than with representation and utility.

We have not realized sufficiently the richness of this kind of play material on the one hand, nor the richness of children's imaginative resources on the other. No adult could have planned a didactic method which could have stimulated children to this sort of activity, but also no such building is found unless favorable conditions are made for it. These include a lavish supply of materials and a program that gives to children firsthand experiences which make them more aware of the world and their place in it. Added to this is an attitude on the part of the teacher that the interest of children in construction is significant and must be protected. A teacher will feel a genuine enthusiasm for the block building program after she or he has watched such development as the preceding material would indicate.

The details of the teaching techniques which help develop profitable use of blocks cannot be discussed here, but the essentials are a recognition of the possibilities in block building, actual respect for and interest in the activity, the provision of space and time for it, and the protection of the children from interruption and encroachment from less interested individuals. Given such conditions and such a teacher attitude, I believe that in any group of healthy children, the progressive development of structures such as these will be found.

Bibliography

Johnson, H. *Children in the Nursery School.* New York: Agathon Press, 1972. Reissued with an introductory essay by Barbara Biber.
Johnson, H. M. *The Art of Block Building.* New York: Bank Street College of Education Publications, 1966 (first published in 1933).

Mary W. Moffitt

3

Children learn about science through block building

Adults who look upon block building as an idle pastime or a childish activity often fail to realize that block building is a lifetime activity. Whether one is an architect planning a building, a delivery person loading a truck, or a homemaker storing groceries in a cupboard, each is handling various units or forms that fit together in different spatial relations and are influenced by balance and stability. So it is for children as they build with blocks!

It is somewhat difficult to isolate science content in block building without overlapping into other content areas such as that of mathematics and geography. Size, shape, area, and volume are related to both scientific and mathematical concepts. When children build a structure or represent the world symbolically with houses, bridges, ramps, and tunnels, they are dealing with geographical concepts as well as with scientific concepts of space, distance, direction, grids, patterns, and mapping.

Meeting the goals of science education

Perhaps it is easier to think about block building as an activity that meets many of the present goals for science education. Today, we are beginning to realize that science content is bet-

51

ter learned through the development of the processes of inquiry such as observing, comparing, classifying, predicting, and interpreting. Block building is a medium that is particularly well adapted for the use of many of these processes. Scientific thinking is stimulated as children discover and invent new forms, compare and classify different sizes and shapes, test out ideas of "What will happen if . . . ?" or, learn to use clues to predict certain outcomes because they have become familiar with the properties of the blocks with which they build.

Learning the properties of blocks

Science education today emphasizes the importance for young children to learn about the properties of matter, and in block building children learn about properties of different kinds of blocks. Each block has certain qualities such as size, shape, and weight, and being three dimensional; it has properties of thickness, width, and length. Children soon learn to differentiate many of these dimensions as they use the blocks in their structures. A block may be seen as similar or dissimilar, depending on how it is to be used in certain positional relationships with other blocks.

Children learn also that a block may be placed flat, on edge, or on end, and the use of these surfaces may be combined to create different characteristics in their structures.

Weight is a factor in learning about size, meaning that some blocks may be heavier than other blocks. The way children grasp a block provides certain tactile interpretations of weight, sometimes inaccurately until they learn to grasp it differently. For instance, if children grasp a block a foot or more long at the end, they may think the block is heavier until they learn to grasp it in the center where it is better balanced. Thus the hand is a fulcrum, and the block is a lever. Many other properties are seen and felt, such as the curvature or angularity of a block, its edges, corners, and surface as the child handles different shapes.

When children become aware of the similarities and dissimilarities of size and shape of various blocks, they tend to match and sort them accordingly. This activity is a form of

Scientific thinking requires regular patterns of thought, and block building stimulates children to develop various ways of systematizing their constructions.

classification that is important for scientific thinking. Putting away blocks according to different dimensions enhances the classification process when children are able to store them on shelves in this manner.

Seeing a block structure as a system

Two large conceptual ideas stressed in science education are those of *systems* and *interactions* that occur within a system. A block building is a system composed of parts that are in equilibrium, and this system is established through the interaction of certain parts that are in balance.

Scientific thinking requires regular patterns of thought, and block building stimulates children to develop various ways of

Children learn to work with a cause-effect approach and learn to predict the stress and strain resulting from the forces of gravity interacting on various parts of their buildings.

systematizing their constructions. As they build, they learn that there are certain sequential patterns that need to be followed when they place different blocks in relationship to one another. Children tend to develop a variety of sequential patterns, which they repeat over and over again. Watch how children establish a pattern as they build. If a child lays two blocks parallel, that child may lay two blocks parallel on top of them, but in an opposite direction. Or that child may set up two blocks, and then bridge them and continue the pattern in developing a vertical system. It is through the production and reproduction of these and many other patterns that a child begins to grasp a concept of the "whole-part" relationship within her or his structure or system.

Reversability is the beginning of logical thinking according to Piaget. A way to observe children's ability to perceive the reverse of their sequential patterns is to suggest that they take down their structure in reverse of their putting it up. You may suggest, "Can you take your building down without it falling down?" and note the awareness of reversability as a child removes the appropriate blocks in reverse order.

Learning about interaction of forces within a system

Equilibrium, balance, and stability are governed by the pull of gravity. When children first start building, they are likely to place blocks one on top of another in haphazard fashion, and of course, the tower soon tumbles over. Watch for the time when children begin to place the blocks in more careful alignment, or when they straighten the sides of the tower with their hands. This indicates that they are aware that some action is necessary if they want to build higher, although they don't understand the concept of center of gravity as a force that is interacting among the blocks of their structure. But children learn quickly to predict when a tower has reached a certain height and becomes unsteady. They learn to look for certain clues about the tower's stability and indicate their awareness by the way they place each additional block or by the way they often extend their fingers in anticipation of the moment of collapse.

Another observation may be made of children's perception of stability. Watch how they test their structure by putting on a block rather gingerly, or by placing it tentatively and then quickly taking it away because they perceive that maximum stability has been reached.

While balance and stability are obtained at first through trial and error, children with experience become quite adept in controlling gravitational forces in different ways for effective building. They learn where to place a block so it will support another block, or they learn the necessity of moving a block slightly to obtain better balance. Gradually, children perceive, too, that a broader base will provide for greater stability when they wish to build higher.

Children learn to deal with disequilibrium through the use of counterbalancing. They learn to do this in different ways. Sometimes they achieve balance through interlocking the different faces of the blocks. Or they learn to use more blocks (more weight) to counterbalance a block, depending on how it is supported.

Many children have a tendency to seek right and left balance as they design their buildings. If they place a block on one side of the structure, they often place a similar block in a similar position on the other side of the structure. To do this selective placing, a child must have developed perception of pattern and ready identification of form similarities.

Children, like scientists, focus attention on the problems of stability and seek ways to build that are successful and satisfying to them. Much stimulation to thinking comes from working out problems that arise from the interaction of forces related to balance and equilibrium. "How may I build higher?" "How will this block fit here?" "What must be done to keep it from falling over?"

Accumulation of experience in building all kinds of structures provides a child with a good idea of what can be done or cannot be done with the material. A child learns to work with a cause-effect approach and learns to predict the stress and strain resulting from the forces of gravity interacting on various parts of a building.

Bridging space is a problem requiring perception of space between two or more blocks.

Learning about space

A block is a form or substance that takes up space either vertically or horizontally, depending on how it is placed. When children build by placing one block upon another, they soon realize that the structure becomes taller. Likewise, a long structure results when blocks are placed end to end in a continuous pattern across the floor. This pattern may continue until limitation is reached in the form of a wall or some other object. Then there must be a change of direction, if the pattern is to be continued.

In developing architectural forms, the child learns to deal with problems of proximity and the relationship of one type of structure to another.

Bridging space is a problem requiring perception of space between two or more blocks. An appropriate-sized block must be selected to fit the space between the blocks, or an adjustment must be made to accommodate the particular block being used to span the space.

Space may be enclosed in different ways, and smaller enclosures may be made within larger enclosures. Children like to put objects in these various-sized enclosures, but they have to learn that what is put into a particular enclosure must be in ratio to the enclosed space. In other words, it cannot be bigger than the area enclosed. Similar problems occur when children wish to push a toy truck or boat under a bridge or tunnel. They must perceive that the object must be in ratio to the defined space under the bridge or tunnel.

As children build, their structures take up more and more space. Sometimes they have to change direction or change the pattern due to the limitations of surface area. Some children tend to build very compactly while others tend to extend their structures in different directions. Some children have great interest in exploring vertical space and want to build high. Teachers, in many instances, become fearful and caution the children not to extend their structure beyond their own height. This limitation curtails the activity and the opportunity to deal with problems encountered in building to greater heights after children have developed some construction skills.

Through construction and dramatic play, children learn that there are certain conditions and limitations in space. Those children who have extensive experiences with block building soon acquire perceptive judgment in dealing with space, and they operate accordingly. They become well aware of the need for caution when a building seems unsteady or that a change of direction is needed. It has been observed that such children seem to exhibit a well-defined sense of self in space as well, and that they can move about delicately balanced structures without knocking them down. They seem to become sensitized in how to move and how to handle the material with ease and self-assurance.

Comparing dimensions by measuring

Many opportunities for comparing length, height, and depth are inherent in block building. Each block may be used as a unit of measurement, and children discover equivalency among the different-sized units. Thus they are able to substitute a larger unit for several smaller units or vice versa.

When a child builds vertically or horizontally, a rope or string may be used to measure the height or length of the construction. The rope in turn becomes a unit of measurement that may be used to compare the block structure to the length and height of other objects in the room. The teacher may indicate "Your building is as long as . . . " or "as high as . . . "

Depth may be measured also when a child builds a high enclosure. "How deep is it?" If the enclosure is large enough, sometimes children like to get into it, and they become the unit of measurement in finding out if it is as deep as they are tall.

Building architectural forms

Architectural forms are readily achieved with blocks. Tunnels, bridges, ramps, and towers are created as blocks are organized into certain positional relationships. The builder soon learns to use the units to make different forms in developing a miniaturized world for using toy cars, trucks, and the like. In developing architectural forms, the child learns to deal with problems of proximity and the relationship of one type of structure to another. Various kinds of buildings assume the approximation of distance and direction in mapping out the reproduction of the larger world. Roadways have direction and are in certain positional relationship to bridges or tunnels. Buildings have certain relationships to roads and other kinds of buildings. Even particular buildings have distinctive characteristics that children attempt to reproduce, such as a garage, a house, or a store.

A ramp is an inclined plane, but it is also considered to be a machine for raising objects from one level to another with a minimum of effort. Children learn the function of the inclined plane when they place a ramp for a roadway or some place of entry for their toys. Use of the ramp enables a child to test its function by pushing the toy up or by letting the toy roll freely down the ramp.

Thinking creatively and scientifically

Invention and discovery are part of scientifc thinking. A successful scientist has a creative mind and creates new forms through finding new relationships among established ideas.

In block building, the material is fluid, providing for infinite possibilities for a child to develop ideas and improvise or create at will, provided, of course, that the child has an adequate number of blocks with which to work and opportunities to use them.

Developing the skills of inquiry through block building seems to be a realistic approach to science content. Usually young children tend to work intuitively, rather than logically. It is better to permit the children to invent explanations for their experiences, as they deal with the concrete materials and manipulate them in different ways. Through exploration, invention, and discovery, children develop ways of thinking about physical phenomena that they encounter in their construction. In this way, they build background information in a meaningful way that will be relative to more complex concepts later on.

Too often children are urged to deal with abstract ideas before they are prepared to do so. All that is accomplished is that the children mouth the words without understanding.

Teachers should not attempt to teach science content formally, but rather they should reinforce what the child has done by the use of a descriptive comment such as, "You have learned how to balance that long block with some smaller ones" or "You have found the right-sized truck to go through your tunnel."

Asking questions judiciously is another way to help children focus on some aspect of their work, for example, "Can you make a ramp for the cars to go into your garage?" or "Where will you put the road?"

It is advisable from time to time to get children to verbalize how they solved a problem in construction by asking, "How did you get those blocks to balance?" or "How did you know where to put the big block?"

Inquiry-centered learning allows children to develop their thinking and can lead learners to discover for themselves what they are ready to understand. It is important, however, for teachers to develop insight into how these processes function for scientific thinking. Furthermore, to be effective, a teacher must be a communicator in these processes, too, when working with children.

Kristina Leeb-Lundberg

4

The block builder mathematician

A child's artistry in—and feeling for—block building is closely related to the true mathematician's view of mathematics as a creative art. The aesthetic pleasure which adult mathematicians experience when they contemplate shape and form and their properties is similar to the pleasure and joy children experience when they build. Blocks give children an entry into a world where objects have predictable similarities and relations. They can be explored and experimented with and, because of their specific shape, be absolutely relied upon. With them, children can produce useful constructions from real life, or pure forms to wonder and marvel at. Unknown to children, structures reflect concise mathematical relations. Children's pleasure in form and structure is mathematical in nature.

Since antiquity, there has been a mystery around geometric shapes and solids, to mathematicians and builders alike. The Greeks discovered that there are only five regular geometric solids. One of them is the cube. No matter how you turn a cube around, it looks the same seen from each of its six different faces. It is uniquely symmetrical. The cube's cousin, the oblong block (in our case, the unit block), also exhibits mysteries of symmetry and regularity. It has a limited number of faces, edges, and corners. Its straightness and elongated form make it into an ideal building material. It has played a very important role in the architecture of both Western and Eastern civilizations. The stone blocks of the pyramids were in the shape of rectangular solids; the Incas used them in their long-lasting

When children build with blocks they establish an experiential foundation of architecture and mathematics. Perhaps a future architect will appear.

structures. The rectangle was put into particularly good use in the Greek temples, where not only the foundation, but the four sides of the temples were rectangular in shape, the front a so-called golden rectangle. In modern life, few buildings can be thought of which do not make a profuse use of the rectangle in the shape of the bricks, the plan of the foundations and the rooms, the forms of the doorways and windows.

So when children build with blocks, they establish an experiential foundation of architecture and mathematics. There is a relational understanding which comes into play when they build, an understanding which is the basis for the study of architecture and mathematics alike. There is a specific individuality and feeling about it as well. Suggest, for example, that two children use ten blocks of the same kind. See what different kinds of structures they make. Perhaps a future architect will appear. Frank Lloyd Wright said in his autobiography that in trying to trace the influences that led him to become an architect, the Froebelian kindergarten blocks he had used in the 1870s were the only things he could be enthusiastic and definite about:

> The smooth, shapely maple blocks with which to build, the sense of which never afterwards left the fingers: so form became feeling. (1932, p. 11)

Children themselves are, in their early years, in what Eileen Churchill calls the "age of comparisons." By an infinite number of comparisons, they find out about the world around them. Their learning is a relationship to form. In order to describe their world, they begin to use the language of mathematics.

An adult definition of mathematics is that it is a study of structures or a study of systematic patterns of relationships. This kind of study is important for general abstract thinking as well. Children's ability to compare one thing with another becomes a key to their mental or cognitive development. We must, therefore, neither overestimate nor underestimate what happens intellectually when children are building with blocks. That is when they are accumulating experience with the almost infinite number of ways in which blocks can be related to one another. To understand it more fully, we will, however, have to extend our knowledge of mathematics per se, as well as of general developmental learning. It is only when we ourselves have a reasonably clear picture of what may (or may not) happen in children's perceptions and conceptions that we can be of most help to children in supporting their intellectual development. Perhaps we will find that the most important thing we can do is to *observe* and, in this process, appreciate and admire the child's accomplishments.

Our knowledge of mathematics as a structure and a language is usually quite inadequate, although this is not likely to be a fault of our own. Many of us were exposed to a type of mathematics teaching and learning that did nothing to make us enthusiastic about the subject.

To most of us, geometry seems mainly to be associated with the naming of regular shapes such as squares, triangles, circles, etc., perhaps including some of the regular solids—cubes, spheres, and so forth—imbued with properties and formulas from a long-forgotten school geometry. This belongs to a type of geometry mathematicians call Euclidean. Euclid's geometry is a geometry of objects and, in the final analysis, is concerned with interrelationships between points, lines, and planes (to children, at their concrete stage, corners, edges, and faces of blocks). It includes a geometry of size, shape, and measurement of height, length, area, volume, angles, etc.

Children, while playing with blocks, perceive and eventually conceptualize Euclidean notions inherent in the blocks and in the structures they build with them, but this happens only gradually. It is not the place where they start out in their geometrical and mathematical concept formation. Their geometric learning through blocks should not be seen in isolation from their general environmental experience.

There are some wider fields of geometry that we have to explore if we want to acquire a broader base for our understanding of the geometric perceptions that children are preoccupied with during their building with blocks, namely the branches of mathematics called topology and projective geometry. Foreign as these terms may seem, they help us to understand the broad learning young children are involved in while they slowly work their way toward Euclidean concepts. It is of particular interest to us here that it is these three geometric systems together—*topology, projective,* and *Euclidean geometry*—that Piaget has used in his explorations of young children's developmental learning about space. Our field of study therefore carries us beyond unit blocks.

The geometric concepts of topology are, on the child's level, based on very fundamental spatial relations. When objects are placed next to one another, children experience nearness (proximity); seriation produces order. Other topological notions are surrounding (enclosure), separation, and the more elastic continuum (the idea that lines and surfaces are continuous and do not only exist in bits and pieces).

Since objects—and their shapes—rarely are seen in full-plane view, projective geometry has been called the geometry of viewpoints. It is concerned with seeing objects from differing sides and angles, or as seen in perspective, from near or far. The differing shapes that shadows make are part of the study of this type of geometry.

It is not difficult to give examples of children's topological experiences. The ideas of inside and outside are part of the concepts of enclosure or surrounding. Everyone is familiar with children's passion for the insides of things: for the opening and closing of boxes; for taking things out of a box, only to put them right back in again and secure the lid tightly, then repeat the whole procedure. Friedrich Froebel, the father of the kindergarten, was the first to document such observations from his work with young children in 1836 (Leeb-Lundberg 1972, p. 152). And in New York in 1973, a restless boy walks into the kindergarten one morning, walks over to the block corner, takes out a few blocks, completely encircles a little floor space for himself, moves one block slightly to the side, walks in, closes the door, and sits quietly for ten minutes. Then he opens the door, goes outside, relaxed and satisfied, to join the other children in play. Even more topological in nature is the wish of five-year-old Tommy in the Adirondacks, who quietly pondering one day, said to his teacher, "I wish I could dig a hole, crawl into it, and pull it into me!" Without the topological notions of inside and outside (in the latter story also elasticity and continuity), stories like these would have no meaning.

And when a girl builds a little house with walls in order to creep into it and sit there with her best friend (perhaps under a table, so she has a good and stable roof for her enclosure,) she again makes the real world conform to her bodily and emotional needs through the topological notion of inside. When she sits on top of a building and the house is under her, she is also very obviously outside it. The richness in her experience is strengthened by the fact that on top of it and under can be

considered Euclidean concepts as well, through the child's beginning learning about directions in space. Whether the foundation of the house is a square, an irregular triangle, or even a
pentagon, makes no difference to her—it is the enclosure that
counts. Her inside and outside relate to anything she may
build: a boat, an airplane, a car, a garage, etc.

In all these instances, the different angles from which children experience their structures (from inside, outside, in front
of, in back of, etc.) make the shapes they contain constantly
change as children move about. The structure will seem different whether they are close to it, or some distance away. The
perspective, as well as the size, changes, and the blocks themselves look different as they turn them around. This all becomes part of the important projective geometric space existing
when an object is not thought of in isolation, but in relation to
a point of view. Children's difficulty in internalizing projective
ideas may be seen in their drawings: houses shown from various points of view concurrently, or a face in profile with two
eyes.

Development and insights

Space in children's minds is never still. Their ideas of space
grow out of the awareness of their own bodies. In this, they are
close to notions of early humans. Some terms used by primitive
people suggest clearly that the body is the source of their spatial concepts. (The word *eye* can indicate *before*, the word *back*
can indicate *behind*, and the word *ground* can indicate *under*.)
Seen this way, a word like *floor* can be looked upon as a directional word for preschool children. They build on it all the time;
it is always at the bottom of their structure and provides the
basis for it. Much later, the notion that change of position can
be related to a fixed reference point becomes central to the idea
of measurement and also to the construction of so-called Euclidean space.

In the preschool, children learn mainly by moving. Their
movements include running, jumping, stretching, lifting, putting down. The block corner may be *far away* in the other end
of the room; they run to get *close* to it, so they can take out the

During the several years of block building, the child goes through a puzzling process in development toward more stable spatial concepts.

blocks and start building. They may stretch *high* in order to make their buildings *tall*. Their towers may be *close to* the wall, or *next to* the window or doll house. They jump *down* from a ramp. The block corner may be *separated from* the entrance door by a bookcase, or be *enclosed by* partitions.

Children do not learn concepts in a vertical fashion. Topological, projective, and Euclidean notions mix from quite early on, although the first basic adjustments infants make seem to be topological in nature: when they relate to the outside of their mothers, to their cribs, to their own bodies with all their miraculous extremities that can stretch or clutch. The topological ideas of being near something (their mother), of being less close to her (separation) become meaningful in terms of subjective, sometimes emotional experiences. Handling of objects leads to a certain knowledge of figures and shapes. Although quite young children may be able to recognize and even name linear shapes such as squares and triangles, the image of these objects in their minds has been proven to be vague. In fact, it has been shown by Piaget that children identify shapes which display topological relationships such as rounded forms more readily than they can identify Euclidean straight shapes. (It is interesting that rounded forms are closer to nature, such as the mother's face and body.)

Block builder mathematicians in the nursery school are, therefore, children who are in what Piaget calls the pre-operational stage or the stage of intuitive reasoning. Their experiences are bound to stay subjective, rather than objective and quantitative, for a long time, in fact, for most of the years that they are block builders. They start out with perceptions which eventually develop into what we call conceptions or concepts. This process depends upon a huge amount of experience they have to go through. For example, in order to be able to put things into classes or categories, at first they are likely to think of a thing in terms of concrete and subjective situations; for example, that is, they define objects descriptively in terms of actions: *a nose is to blow, a block is to build*. The development of what we call geometric intuition becomes an activity. It begins with adaptive actions which become linked with the object, and next assimilate the object into functional structures. As the number of distinctions between objects gets larger, the number of categories increases. They start talking about blocks without subjective descriptions and eventually about smaller classes of blocks which they give specific names such as rectangles and triangles.

When children come to kindergarten at about the age of five, most of them are, in their reasoning, still guided by perception and imagery, not conceptions. Their reasoning is in many ways static and immobile. They cannot use it in a flexible way. They move slowly, in some ways, toward an ability to operate with mathematical and geometric concepts out of concrete situations (the earliest concept being that of number). For a general introduction to Piaget's theory, see Wadsworth (1979). Their ability to truly operate does not come until they are six or seven; in other cases, not until they reach nine or ten. It will take even longer before space becomes detached in their minds from the concrete and affective, that is, becomes abstract.

During the several years of their block building period, children go through a puzzling process in their development toward more stable spatial concepts. Although their building activity with blocks is very important, we must be aware that rudimentary skills in making use of shapes (fitting them, matching them) exist in them without having much understanding of the facts that underlie these figures. They must, in order to move into the so-called operational stage of geometric thought, pass beyond the stage of imagery as a basis of representational thought, and they must learn to appreciate the significance of the transformations that take place as they classify objects, put them in order of size which, by being rearranged, yield first one perceptual structure, then another. In this period, perceptual space develops far more rapidly than conceptual space. It can even reach a projective or quasi-metric level which Euclidean space has barely begun. Therefore, when conceptions begin to develop, perceptions exist alongside them. Children go through what has been called a period of disequilibrium.

Generally, children's ability to talk about what they are doing is behind their ability to do. Gradually, language and action begin to merge. It is an increasing awareness of the significance of their experience which brings the child to naming or accepting a word given by an adult at the right moment. The following words are learned at the preschool level for the simplest relationships: *up, down, over, under, above, below, before, behind.* They seem necessary for children to fix their attention on what they stand for. It is difficult for children to discuss spatial relationships without using these words. Most preschool children also understand the words *on top* and *behind;* at the age of five, the terms *backward* and *forward* are understood by many, according to one study. But only 60 percent showed that they understood the difference between *tiny* and *huge,* and less than one-half could show that they understood the difference between *far* and *near* (Lovell 1964, p. 93).

It is the actions that are performed on the objects that bring about a more conceptual space. For this reason, the building activity with blocks (and other real-life material) is so important. When children build up a repertoire of actions, they accumulate experience of their effect. In Piaget's language, thought arises from the interiorization of actions. Geometrical thought per se is a system of internalized actions. As soon as children have some ability to represent to themselves in thought spatial relationships that are not directly observable, their actions build up systems of mental operations with which, when they coordinate them with one another, they can interpret the world better. It is interesting to note that children's first tentative efforts in block building are efforts to make representations of real things in the physical world. Friedrich Froebel observed this and called these structures—of houses, furniture, etc.—which children make "Forms of Life."

When children are able to perform operations, they are able to think about mental processes in a new way. They become able, specifically, to do what Piaget calls conserve, which will be discussed later, and are able to reverse their thinking, that is, go backward to the starting point and think through the process.

How young children may struggle with the idea of reversibility—when they have not yet reached the developmental stage in which they can internalize the actions preceding this concept—is illustrated by the child who, while visiting the zoo, was taken up by one flight of stairs and down by another. The next day, when visiting the zoo again, she was taken up by the stairs she had previously come down. She protested that these were "going down" stairs and the others were "going up" stairs.

When children build, they constantly accumulate experiences with the different ways in which objects can be related to one another. This becomes the foundation for a multitude of mathematical concepts, not only that of number.

Another story is told about a seven-year-old who had been taken for a long circular walk through the woods. When they were almost home again, the boy was shown a strawberry patch. The following day, the boy tried to walk with his mother from the house directly to the patch, but he was unable to do so. Instead, he had to make the circular journey all through the woods as on the day before, until he again came across the strawberries. This child relied all the time on a chain of associations and memories. He was not able, yet, to reverse his thinking (Lovell 1964, pp. 92–93).

True reversibility means, according to Piaget, that when children think or internalize their actions, they are also able to reverse their thinking about what they did, that is, go backward to the point where they began and think through their experience. The children in the just related stories could not do this and are, therefore, said to be in the preoperational stage. From the age of seven on, a great change in power of reversibility of thinking takes place.

These rather surprising stories about young children's thinking ought, again, to put us more in the observer's place than in the teachers. It is very important to realize the psychological development children are going through, so that we do not mistake some half knowledge of the developmental process of mathematical concept formation and try to teach them things which they can only, in the privacy of their own mind, go through with the aid of a multitude of practical experiences. Research has made it abundantly clear that concept formation cannot be forced. All children have, in their own time, to pass through certain developmental stages in their conceptual development, related to their chronological and mental age and experience. For some children, the process takes a long time; for others, it happens more quickly.

With care, the blocks can, however, be used to find out whether children are able to analyze a construction they have made, in order to find out whether they can reverse the process they used in building it. They can be sympathetically asked to look at it carefully and see how it was put together, then take it to pieces and reconstruct it. The degree of difficulty will, of course, depend upon how elaborate the original construction was. It might be interesting to observe whether they sort their blocks, for example, according to shape or size.

To fully realize the amount of intuitive learning that is involved when children play with blocks, we need also to be aware of what Piaget calls conservation. Up to six, seven, or even eight years of age, most children do not appear to understand that the amount or quantity (that is, of blocks, raisins, buttons, clay) stays the same, regardless of changes in shape, positions, or rearrangement. (Children reach conservation of number first.) If we consider the set of unit blocks, another surprising conclusion can therefore be drawn from Piaget's experiments with children. Four- to six-year-olds (sometimes even older children) are apt to believe that, once they have taken all the blocks off the shelves and built a large, spread-out construction on the floor, they now have more blocks than when the same blocks were stored in a compact way on the shelves. In other words, they center their attention on only one aspect of the situation at a time; in this case, the floor space the blocks occupy, rather than the actual amount of pieces involved. They cannot conserve the amount.

When children build, they constantly accumulate experiences with the different ways in which objects can be related to one another. This becomes the foundation for a multitude of mathematical concepts, not only that of number. Conservation, for example, relates also to the geometric concepts of length, area, and volume. The fact that these concepts are generally not reached until after kindergarten age does not belittle the children's kindergarten experience. Their pre-mathematical practice as block builders becomes very significant, both to them as experimenters and discoverers and to us as observers. With age and experience, children gradually come to appreciate the mathematical meaning of their own actions through their constant rearranging of the materials they use in their constructions, whether they are houses, ships, towers, or highways.

Mathematical concepts

Developmental examples follow under the headings of the main mathematical concepts with which they deal. In many of these instances, we will find that the children's activities touch on the problem of whether amount, length, etc., stays the same, no matter what the position of the objects. In fact, they deal, in regard to the set of blocks, with what a mathematician would call all the possible permutations (or arrangements) of the material. This again relates, in the cases of young children, to movement. Either the object is moved around, or their own body moves in relation to the object.

Length

When children begin to work with blocks, they usually put them together flat on the floor, a few pieces at a time, first one block, then another, and then another. Later, blocks laid end to end become a road or a railroad track. When they discover that they can pile the blocks on top of each other, building *up*, *high*, this is quite a surprise for them. The repetitive activity of arranging blocks in towers and rows can absorb children for a long time. To lay one block upon another may, to some children, be a simpler process than to place them next to one another in a line (although two-year-old children have been observed to build towers and rows the first month they were given blocks to play with).

In these beginning activities, the topological notions are the basic challenge to the child: nearness (next to one another), separation (apart from one another), and order (one after the other). Eventually these ideas merge with the concepts of length (the concept of length including the horizontal width and the vertical height and depth.

Before children come to school, they experience comparisons rather than names of actual lengths, such as *this is longer than that* or *that is higher than this*. These expressions about so-called inequality of length are associated with many experiences ranging, possibly, from the length of their fingers to the height of mountains. Children usually refer to their own body or to their body in relation to other objects. They experience that what is high or tall is relative—their block towers may be high, but so is the Empire State Building. To say that something is longer or shorter is easier to the child, and comes earlier, than to say it is *the same length* or *as long as* (equality of length). From their play and by watching grown-ups, children may also experience that a stick can be shortened by breaking it, or that blocks can be joined to other blocks to make longer tracks or trains, or, as in the following case, submarines.

> Six-year-old Tommy was asked about the submarine he had made. He said it was for one boy inside and one on top. When asked how he could make the inside large enough for the two boys, he immediately suggested making the model longer by adding one more block at each end.

The individual blocks, of course, exhibit simple length relationships as well:

> During block building I asked a four-year-old, Kelli, to find a block that was longer than the one I placed on the floor. The block on the floor was a half unit or square. She selected a double unit.

One of Piaget's experiments has shown that four-year-old children do not use the word *straight* and have difficulty constructing a straight line. When asked to make one, they instead constructed a wavy or curved line. This can also be observed when children work with unit blocks. At about the age of six, the child, however, sights along the line from one end and is, therefore, able to make the line straight. The relative ease with which the wide unit blocks can be fitted together gives children working with them experiences with straight lines, however.

A conceptual problem they are involved with is the equivalence of length no matter what the shape or angles of the line. When children build railroad tracks and use curved as well as oblong unit blocks, the following lengths will be about equivalent:

In specific experiments by Piaget, it has been shown that children have quite some difficulty realizing that the length of two identical lines (or blocks, representing lengths) put in different position, remain the same:

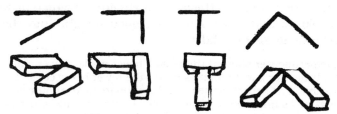

Length can also mean perimeter, i.e., an outline of a foundation for a building. In the following cases, both perimeters, as measured by unit blocks, are the same, although visually they may appear different:

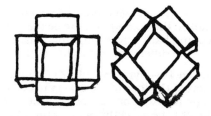

It is not until about the age of seven, and sometimes later, that children are able to conserve length, that is, realize that the length is the same no matter what the arrangement of the individual blocks used.

To the concept of length belongs the idea of being able to measure it. For measurement of length, conservation of length is necessary. The child also needs eventually to understand that a whole consists of a number of parts added together and that length can be measured in terms of other lengths, that is, through the repeated application of a unit of measure. The essence of measurement is again *comparison;* that one thing is being compared with another called a unit of measure. This unit of measure is arbitrary. The unit blocks can be measured in terms of other unit blocks, but they can also be measured in terms of handspans, thumbprints, or straws put end to end. Conceptually, measurement is the synthesis of division into parts and of what Piaget calls iteration (repetition) of the unit.

Young children have no idea at all of lengths in terms of other lengths. One Piagetian experiment studied children's spontaneous measurement at different ages. It will be quoted at length, since it is one of the few experiments in which he made use of blocks and since it gives a good insight into the developmental levels of children:

> The experimenter showed the child a tower made of twelve blocks and a little over 2 feet 6 inches high—the tower being constructed on a table. The experimenter told the child to make another tower "the same as mine" on another table about 6 feet away, the table top being some 3 feet lower than that of the first table. There was a large screen between the model and the copy but the child was encouraged to "go and see" the model as often as he liked. He was also given strips of paper, sticks, rulers, etc., and he was told to use them if his spontaneous efforts ceased, but he was NOT told how to use them. The following stages were observed:
>
> (a) up to about 4½ yrs. of age there was visual comparison only. The child judged the second tower to be the same height as the first by stepping back and estimating height. This was done regardless of the difference in heights of the table tops.
>
> (b) this lasted from 4½–7 yrs. roughly. At first the child might lay a long rod across the tops of the towers to make sure they were level. When he realized that the base of the towers were not at the same height, he sometimes attempted to place his tower on the same table as the model. Naturally, that was not permitted. Later, the children began to look for a measuring instrument, and some of them began using their own bodies for this purpose. For example, the span of the hands might be used, or the arms, by placing one hand on top of the model tower and the other at the base and moving over from the model to the copy, meanwhile trying to keep the hands the same distance apart. When they discovered that this procedure was unreliable, some would place, say, their shoulder against the top of the tower (a chair, or stool might be used) and would make a spot on their leg opposite the base. They would then move to the second tower to see if the heights were the same.
>
> (c) from 7 years onwards there was an increasing tendency to use some symbolic object (e.g. a rod) to imitate size. Very occasionally a child built a third tower by the first and carried it over to the second: this was permitted. More frequently, though, he used a rod that was exactly the *same length* as the model tower was high. (Lovell 1964, pp. 107–108)

In the latter cases, there was an experience of equality in matching identical lengths—an intelligent beginning comparison. It was found, however, that children sometimes used a stick which was shorter than the tower. It was applied the necessary number of times. The height of the model tower was then found by repeatedly using a shorter stick as a means of measurement. This, of course, meant that the concept of measurement of length was finally formed.

It is of particular interest that some of the children began to use their own bodies as instruments for measuring or in some way related it to the height of the tower. Our whole standard system of measure, the yard system, originated with people using different parts of our bodies as measures. This again shows that the children instinctively are on the same stage as early civilization.

To build a tower as tall as you are is a good means of finding equal lengths. Games using handspans, paces, feet, or body lengths (children stretched out in a line on the floor) to measure the length of a construction or the room are enjoyable activities for them. Sometimes, perhaps, unit blocks can be used as units of measure (no stress on this language with the children!) to find out how long or how tall a building is. More advanced children could *make* a measuring stick, calibrated according to blocks and painted: a story stick with which you measure the stories in the building. Mathematicians recommend that children begin to learn about measurements using this kind of arbitrary unit, so well-suited to their subjective experiences. To make the activities richer, children who are ready can first estimate or guess how many blocks or handspans will be needed. The following example shows how five- and six-year-olds use their bodies for comparison in finding out about height and blocks as arbitrary units of measure. Dick and Johnny are five; Bill and Jonathan, six:

> Dick and Johnny built towers. Johnny said his was the highest. He measured his by standing up. Dick also stood up. He said he was as high as Johnny and his tower higher than Dick's. Dick then tried to build his up higher, but Bill and Jonathan built towers, too, and Bill said they were both the same. They discussed this and quadruple units were used to prove who was right.

Beginning mesurement can be learned through the comparison of a child's construction with other objects in the room as well. A piece of string or rope beside the structure can become a unit of measurement. Comparative terms can be used as the length of string is matched to various objects: *Your building is longer than the table* or *higher than the shelf.* In another case, a question can be asked such as *find something that is as long as your block.* Next, measure it to see how nearly correct the child was.

When using the blocks, the matching of smaller pieces to larger ones (constantly occuring in the building of walls, for example) involves a certain intuitive measurement of length (or matching of size). Thus, if the quadruple unit is compared with the unit block, it is found to be equal to four unit blocks, or two units equal one double unit:

> Erick, who was building an airport, could only find double units on the storage shelves. The double units were not long enough to reach across the walls of the airport to make a roof. He took two of the double units over to Ricky and said, "I'll let you have these two blocks if you give me one of your long blocks. Look, you can use these two blocks in your wall—they'll just fit where you have this long one." They traded the blocks. Later Ricky offered all his quadruple units for every two double units which Erick gave him.

This kind of experience leads, of course, in the direction of fractional concepts: halves, fourths, and so on. This is further discussed in the section "Some mathematical features of the Pratt blocks."

Area and volume

Children frequently enclose area in their play. An outline form is one of the simple beginning structures they make. We encountered this idea in the first topological examples of insides. Every block house has a foundation which is an outline of its area. Its shape is instinctive with the child. It does not have to be square or rectangular—an odd-shaped house, such as a pentagonal or L-shaped one—may be even more interesting. In all cases, the foundation determines the size of the house, the size of the areas of the walls and the roof.

The word *area* may, on a child's level, be defined as amount of surface or, in the case of the outline of a house, a car, or a boat that the child builds, simply as amount of floor space.

Before their block building stage, children encounter many situations in which an amount of surface of something comes within their perception. Their mattress is covered with sheets and a blanket. They see floors, doors, windows, table tops, tiles, and blocks which all display a surface. At the easel, they cover up a sheet of paper with poster paint. Slowly they build in their minds some notion of area or size of surface. They notice that some surfaces are larger than others, or that there is more room on some surfaces than on others. They love to work on the surface they call the floor. They feel its bigness. They discover that areas not only have different size, but also different shape. Comparing two tables of different shape, but of about the same area, they may again center on one aspect of the problem at a time, such as the length, and say that the longer surface is also the bigger. Even when they have reached the concept of area, they, like some adults, may not formulate insight very well, but say that this table is bigger, when in reality they mean that its area is bigger.

Preschool children gain many useful experiences with unit blocks which will give them an operational understanding of area later. In their continual experimentation with them, they find out which surfaces fit well together, which blocks make the best walls or roofs, and which surfaces balance best. They find out that the blocks with the largest surface make the best foundations for their structures and that some of the blocks with smaller surfaces can, if joined together, fit on top of the larger surfaces. It will take a long time, however, before they can calculate the area of, let us say, a rectangle. Their ideas will eventually have to apply to an area which is either outlined (a foundation, a doorway, a window frame) or an area covered up with blocks. They have to be able, as with length, to conserve area, no matter what its shape or the arrangement of the individual blocks. In other words, they have to be able to assimilate the fact that the following blocks could cover the same amount of surface:

As children cover a floor space or build up a wall, they are often working with patterns.

Because of the regular properties of the blocks, there is opportunity for recurring experiences which lead toward conservation of area. Most of these experiences refer to surfaces which are covered up by blocks. Some of them refer to individual blocks. Single blocks placed in different positions like the ones below will, to begin with, appear different to children. They are apt to believe that one of them is larger—or smaller—depending on whether they center their attention on the height or the width of the block, for example.

When children are building they may, by chance, put triangular halves together into squares or rectangles:

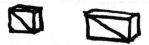

On another occasion, the same pieces may be joined together in the opposite way to form, let us say, a rooftop:

An interesting transformation has now taken place, in that the two smaller triangles have made one larger triangle. (The area, of course, is still the same.)

One Piagetian experiment used two similar triangular shapes, cut out of a cardboard square, in order to investigate the child's specific understanding. The child was asked to make a larger triangle out of the two smaller ones. It was found that five- and six- year-olds tended to believe that the new triangle was bigger than the original square. Six- to seven-year olds made better judgments, although they could only formulate them intuitively. From about seven on, however, children conserved area and gave good reasons why they felt that the area had not changed.

While going through experiences which lead toward the concept, children have unconcerned fun with areas of all kinds. As usual, their involvement in mathematics is unknowing and total as they build houses, garages, airports, barns, and stables. At the same time as they cover a floor space or build up a wall, they are often working with patterns. A simple pattern may be the one made by putting unit blocks together. Their patterns are often symmetrical and show that they perceive the area relationships that appear among the blocks:

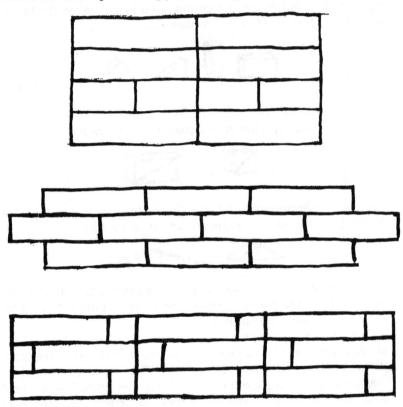

In the following unusual and balanced arrangement the double units are framed in by quadruple units and the total area is well defined:

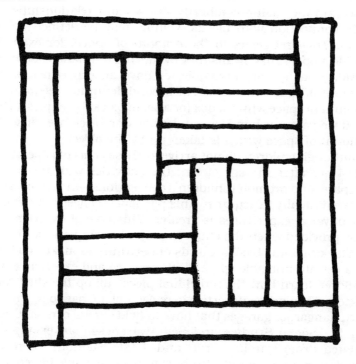

The beauty and the wonder of fitting shapes so exactly is here the child's main interest.

The repeated application of one or more shapes to cover a surface is, in mathematics, called a tesselation, as in the wall patterns below. In the act of covering up, the child is intuitively using the half and double units as units of measure for the total surface.

On occasion, some children may be asked specific questions. Begin by limiting the number of blocks used to ten or twelve squares or unit blocks. Then ask: "How many differently shaped bathroom floors can you lay out with these blocks?" Or children may be invited to experiment with the blocks by constructing rectangular or square forms of various shapes and sizes. It can be pointed out to them that whether these figures are put horizontally or vertically, they still make rectangular shapes.

It is easy to notice how children, when handling the blocks, also gain increasing familiarity with volume relationships.

In connection with blocks, volume may be defined in two ways. The first refers to the *amount of space*, for example, inside a box. (This means that by moving our hands about the inside of a box or cubbyhole we have an experience of the amount of space inside it.) The second definition refers to the amount of space which a box (or a set of blocks) occupies. (That is, if we pass our hands around a box or a block, we sense the amount of space which is taken up by the object.)

Although children do not arrive at these concepts operationally until after the age of ten, the activities with the blocks prepare (and promote) children's conceptions—in fact, because of the difficulty in acquiring this particular concept, their need for physical experiences is greater. This type of experience is also provided when the children play with sand and water.

Stacking away blocks affords opportunity to make good use of a certain available space. With practice and experience, the children learn how the individual pieces fill up the shelf completely. They make airports where each plane has to fit into its own hangar, or garages that have to hold several cars. In Chapter 5, "Social Studies and Self-Awareness," an example is quoted (from Caroline Pratt and Jessie Stanton) where the children are struggling with how to make a stable big enough for a horse:

> A toy horse, returned to school by someone and left on the window seat, was instantly seen by Diana. I said she could have it when she made a stable for it. She and Elizabeth, a new child this year, both began to build. Elizabeth made a tiny construction, but could not put the horse into it. It did not occur to her to change the size of the stable. Diana, on the other hand, having built a large stable with a low roof, after several attempts to force the horse in, removed the blocks composing the roof, made the walls higher, and replaced the roof. She then tried to put into words what she had done, saying, "Roof too small." I gave her the words "high" and "low," and she went about the room smiling and repeating the explanation to the other children (Pratt and Stanton 1926, pp. 30–31).

This example shows well how children are working in more

than one dimension when volume relationships are involved, and how they constructively approach one variable at a time (first height, then width). The activity may also come up when children find the volume of the inner space of, for example, a well they have built by discovering the number of unit blocks that can fill it. To build houses and other objects also helps the children to perceive that a structure takes up a certain amount of room in space.

It must be remembered that volume is puzzling to a child, as illustrated in the following example:

> Three children made towers. They counted the number of blocks in each and found that the highest tower did not have the most blocks.

In another case, a teacher observed two five-year-olds who were trying to decide which was the bigger of two model cars. The dimensions of each were so similar that at long last they put them on the scale, in order to find out by weight which one was the larger.

One teacher reports how on occasion she gave to five-year-olds problems such as the following: "Make a wall that is four blocks long, two blocks high, and one block thick, or "Make a wall that is two blocks deep," or "Make a box that is two blocks square." At the preoperational stage, children approach problems best one at a time. Her first suggestion is too hard for most five-year-olds, although it could provide a challenge for some. A simpler task may be to ask children to make equivalences of various blocks, to make up a quadlong with smaller blocks.

Number

We have found, then, that young children's ideas of size and shape and their possible internal equivalences are mixed up, or in a state of disequilibrium, in regard to length, area, and volume. They slowly move, during their block building stage, toward a state of equilibrium in regard to the concept of number. The geometric experiences children have in block building are most important. In addition, the concept of number should be approached through a multitude of experiences, using a great variety of experiences with diversified materials: buttons, shells, pine cones, acorns, pegs, spoons, straws, dishes, etc.

Still, number experiences are constantly inherent in the use of blocks. A prerequisite for the development of the idea of number is a beginning appreciation that some sets of things are smaller than others, some larger, and that some are the same size. These ideas of equivalence and inequivalence are met within the blocks, mainly in regard to length, area, and volume. This fact, however, undoubtedly helps strengthen the ideas of more and less, also when it comes to sets, groups, or piles of discrete objects or blocks.

> Before Susan (five and one-half years old) started to build she sorted out the different shapes and sizes and put them into separate piles.

As the child takes all the half unit triangular blocks and stacks them, she or he eventually comes to think of all these blocks together and, after some time, forms the concept of a set or class of all the smallest blocks. The child may also come to perceive that the set of unit blocks contains more blocks than the set of triangular blocks, or pillars, and so on.

Other simple experiences of quantity with the blocks are when children ask for more blocks to build with, many more! They might add that they need them because they do not have enough blocks to make their tower high. When asked about how many blocks they used in a large structure, they may not necessarily count them, but simply say they used *a lot*—a good beginning and ancient quantitative word. Other ancient and similar quantitative words are *heap, pile, stack,* and *mound.* Many of their experiences, then, are of a very basic quantitative nature.

Soon, children make efforts to count. After all, most people in their surroundings seem to think that this is the main (or only) approach toward learning number! However, the process of learning numbers is more complex and interesting than that. It develops in stages. It *does* include counting, but this is not all. A child may be able to count and still have no real concept of numbers. The ideas of *more, less,* and *the same as* are more basic.

The fact that a child may be able to count and still not be able to conserve an amount when it appears in a new configuration has been convincingly demonstrated by Piaget and his fol-

Blocks give opportunities for sorting and classifying, for counting and ordering; therefore, they become valuable material in the process of establishing the concept of number.

lowers. A typical Piagetian experiment with the unit blocks would be of the following type: The child makes a row of, for example, five blocks on the floor. He lays out another row next to it with the same number of blocks in it. He is then asked to check the number of blocks by matching them, i.e., putting them into one-to-one correspondence, so that he is absolutely sure the two rows contain the same number of blocks. Then, the teacher spreads out the blocks in one of the rows, so that the simple visual correspondence is lost. The child up to six or even seven when asked usually no longer agrees that the two rows still contain the same number of blocks. His perception leads him to believe the amount in the spread-out row is now larger—that is, he centers his attention on one variable of the problem, namely the new and larger space the blocks occupy. He cannot yet fathom that a number stands for a class or a set of things irrespective of the arrangements of the things within the set.

Another important property of numbers is that they can be

compared with one another and put in order of magnitude. By the age of three or four, children have an intuitive grasp of ordering (shown through their play with nesting toys and by putting graduated rings on sticks). They need to know that the number three is greater than two, but less than four; and that six comes between five and seven. Children, therefore, need a great deal of experience in ordering, that is, in arranging a series of things according to their numerical or size differences. Piaget has shown that up to the age of about five, children are unable to make a series or a set of five or six or seven blocks of increasing length. At about six, they begin to put things in order by using a process of trial and error, but if a block is omitted, it becomes difficult for them to put it into the right place in the series or in the order they are trying to establish. However, at seven, children can take the shortest block, then the next shortest, and so on.

To some children, ordering is very difficult. They need, therefore, practice in putting blocks and things in order of size, that is—in regard to the blocks—from the half unit to the quadruple unit (although, with this small number of pieces, the problem is easier). They need also to do this in reverse, starting with the big, instead of the little block.

Children have not achieved the full idea of number until they have synthesized, in their own mind, the two ideas of grouping into sets (classification) and ordering of sets (seriation). For example, if the blocks are stairs, they may be able to say how many stairs a doll has climbed when it reaches a certain step on the staircase. They come to understand the cardinal and ordinal meanings of numbers together. In this period of disequilibrium, however, the two concepts do not always coincide. They can, therefore, be at the concrete-operational stage of thinking in one aspect, but not in another.

It is because of this developmental process, then, that children need a great deal of experience of a diverse nature in order to establish the number concept. Blocks give opportunities for sorting and classifying, for counting and ordering; therefore, they become valuable material in this process. Almost daily practice with equivalent sets, for example, takes place when children make games of putting blocks away or devise ways of pushing their loads to shelves: "Let's carry piles of five today," and so on.

In the following examples, it has to be remembered that the counting alone is not sufficient for the establishment of the final concept:

> Jonathan counted how many blocks he had used. The rest of the children got interested and also counted theirs.
>
> Mary put seven unit blocks down. She said it was a street. She next put four double units upright next to four of her unit blocks. They were houses along her street. She counted the houses: "One, two, three, four." She counted the rest of the blocks in the street and said, "I need three more houses."

Some mathematical features of the Pratt blocks

Caroline Pratt called her blocks "free materials." In doing so, she was justifiably reacting to the rigid didactic use of Montessori and Froebelian materials in her days:

> . . . in calling these materials *free* materials I can best distinguish them from the materials of the kindergarten and the Montessori schools. Their uses are various. They are not designed for some specific educational purpose of an adult, but are incidental to child life and child purpose. (Pratt 1917, p. 13)

After the misconceptions that had made the early American kindergarten stagnant, she became one who revitalized the Froebelian concept of learning through self-activity, so that it is, still to this day, very much alive.

The very fact that a whole section of this book is devoted to the mathematical development children go through while building with blocks reflects, however, our desire to understand children's cognitive learning in all its aspects.

The variety of size and accompanying flexibility in their use are, of course, the basic factors in the child's satisfaction in building with blocks. The original shapes and sizes were undoubtedly selected because of their volumetric relationships and consequent usefulness for making intricate constructions. Most larger blocks in the set can be replaced in volume by putting together other blocks. The set consists of a comparatively large number of unit blocks and fewer quadruple blocks. This forces users to substitute several unit blocks, for example, for one quadruple block when the supply of large blocks is exhausted. Most of the solids in the set have the common property of equivalence in width and thickness. This makes them useful in displaying equivalence relations, an important class of relations in mathematics.

The basic piece in the set is the one which is traditionally called the unit block. This is the most commonly occurring block in the set, to which most of the others are related. In the set of Pratt blocks, we then have quarter units, half units, units, double units, and quadruple units (for pictures, see Appendix 2). These pieces, when matched, display fractional relationships easily seen when put together lengthwise, as in this pattern, where sets of the smaller blocks are matched against the quadruple unit (sometimes called the quadlong). In relation to the quadlong halves, fourths, eighths, and sixteenths appear:

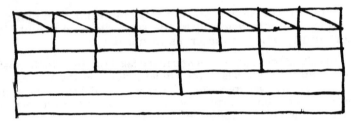

The square block is traditionally called the half unit. However, mathematically the pillars also can be looked upon as halves of the unit block:

Another way of creating a unit block is with two of the large triangles, which then become halves of the unit block:

Or a unit block can be made with two of the small ramps:

Mathematically, there is a richness in seeing halves of the same thing in so many different ways. It also provides a good experience toward the idea of conservation of quantity, since it is inherent in the very material that each of these halves is equivalent to every other:

Blocks that represent fractions in the set, however, have to be seen in relation to the unit block in any configuration. The following shapes show another way of seeing halves (also thirds and fourths) of rectangular areas:

Equivalence of volume is, of course, inherent in these and other configurations. If two half units are put on top of each other, they are still equivalent to the unit block, although visually the shape (or amount of wood) now looks different:

The same applies to many other structures that can be made with the blocks. Four small triangles put on top of each other contain the same amount of wood as one unit block. Two small triangles on top of each other are equivalent to one half unit; eight small triangles on top of each other are equivalent to one double unit, sixteen to one quadruple unit:

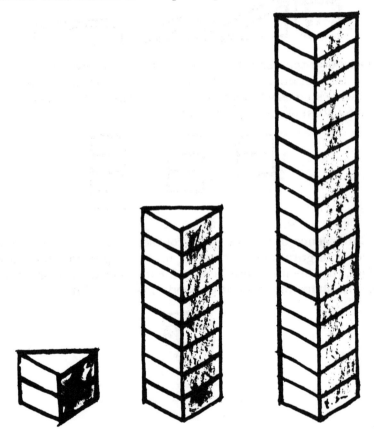

To prove these last equivalent relations, it is only necessary to match the triangular pieces lengthwise with the oblong blocks with which they are compared.

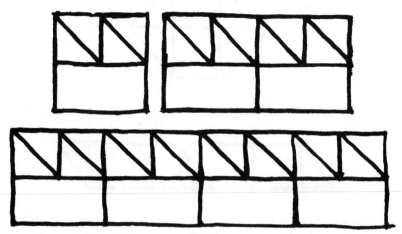

This approach to a mathematical proof is legitimate to a mathematician—a proof being what makes *sense* at a particular level of intellectual development.

There are many opportunities for discoveries about shapes when the blocks are used. A multitude of configurations appear from children's spontaneous arrangements. Four of the small triangles can make a square:

Four of the large triangles can make a rhombus:

Two squares and four small triangles a hexagon:

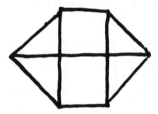

Two triangles joined to a square or rectangle make a parallelogram:

Or two small triangles and a square create a trapezoid. (It does not matter whether the long side of the trapezoid is at the top or bottom. In the former case, the children may call it a boat).

Shapes and forms in one, two, or three dimensions can be illustrated indefinitely through the mathematical model which the set of blocks constitutes. It is sufficient to end with the following example, which is also written out as an arithmetical statement in order to show the implications (in children's constructions) for later formal work with whole numbers and fractions:

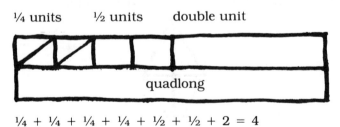

$$\frac{1}{4} + \frac{1}{4} + \frac{1}{4} + \frac{1}{4} + \frac{1}{2} + \frac{1}{2} + 2 = 4$$

These arithmetical facts are inherent whether the blocks are put end to end, as in the above picture, or used freely in building, such as in the ship below, which is made out of the same blocks as above. The ship, then, is equivalent to the quadruple unit in regard to length, area, and volume:

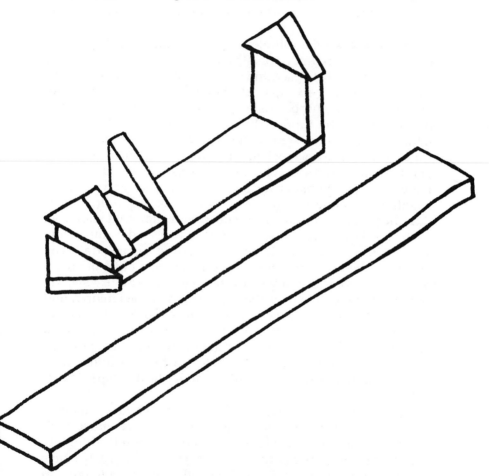

This illustrates Piaget's theory of conservation, which is one of the main mathematical experiences which children go through when they are building with these blocks.

The teacher

It has been stressed throughout this chapter how interesting and rewarding it can be to study the perceptions (and conceptions) of children's minds as applied through blocks. They develop ideas about mathematics with form—that is what opens their minds.

Round blocks (like cylinders), for example, roll. When children see them rolling, something happens in their minds. Their conception of space and geometric form moving through space changes (try to catch it!). Square or rectangular blocks can, in contrast, only be pushed. There is no momentum in the square itself. The kind of blocks we give to children determines, in a certain sense, the type of creative imagination which comes into play when they build with them. At some point in the child's development, a gradual introduction of more blocks, or a greater variety of shapes, intuitively becomes a mathematical need and a responsibility of the adult.

In the type of informal, open-ended education that should go on in the kindergarten, an understanding of the underlying structure of whatever learning is going on is vital. The teacher's role regarding block building is not a difficult one, if one knows what is inherent in the material. The teacher will then know how to extend the experiences of the children and ask the right questions or pose some new problem. Of course, in this process, the adult needs to know where the individual child is—this is what developmental learning is all about. Encouragement and appreciation help teachers to understand and have a right attitude toward children who develop at different tempos.

The teacher can, through questions, help children discover how things differ and how (and where) they resemble each other. This becomes, in all its aspects, true relational thinking, the essence of mathematics as a structure. The teacher may take pictures of a construction from different angles in order to bring out projective geometric aspects and let children look and make comments. However, children are constantly involved in nonverbal questions of their own, and they cannot generally see or talk with the same detail as an adult. The things that children actually understand are the ones that are of real value

Our aim for mathematician block builders should be to make it possible for them to use their mathematical and architectural creativity so that their interest and spontaneous pleasure in what they are doing is kept alive.

to them and which they can use in future constructions.

It is better for the teacher not to guess what a building represents. Children's purposes are sometimes better served if the teacher is as ambiguous as the children are. If a name is given to their structure, accept it, no matter how incongruous it may seem. The true purpose of children's buildings is not always representational, but experimental, to find out what the material will do and what one can do with it. On the other hand, a teacher may be deceived because a child can use the appropriate word and still have no idea about the concept it relates to.

However, language does play a very important role, since most concepts are developed with some kind of verbalization. In order to understand how things are related, children must be given words that describe likenesses and differences. This specialized, broad, mathematical vocabulary provides them with further means for experimenting, thinking, and reasoning about relationships: each new word may pinpoint a relationship. This still does not mean that we should force children to verbalize about their constructions. Meaningful language development comes naturally and often represents a summation of some new insight based on innumerable experiences. The language of the adult is truly accepted by children only if it lies within the circle of their experiences and ideas. This is, again, where our listening and observing becomes so important. What children do with blocks shows an extraordinary variety, and so do their verbal exchanges about their constructions. The mathematical language from the adult has to be provided at the right time, so that it helps a concept to develop appropriately—if it is too soon, it may hinder the development of the concept.

We have to remember that children develop these concepts as if coming into a cave. They don't know what is in it. The cave is empty—only after they come in do they start to discover. There may be a square, a triangle, and a cylinder there. They experience each of these individually. They are surprised at what is in the cave. They start absorbing the dimensions of the objects in their mind. From the impressions they receive, they intuitively start building. Through children's perceptions, intuition, and activity, they are lead toward the concepts. Their driving force is curiosity.

Our aim for mathematician block builders should be to make it possible for them to use their mathematical and architectural creativity so that their interest and spontaneous pleasure in what they are doing is kept alive.

Bibliography

Churchill, E. M. *Counting and Measuring: An Approach to Number Education in the Infant School.* Toronto: University of Toronto Press, 1961.

Dienes, Z. P., and Golding, E. W. *Exploration of Space and Practical Measurements.* New York: Herder and Herder, 1966.

Holloway, G. E. T. *An Introduction to the Child's Conception of Space.* New York: Humanities Press, 1967.

Johnson, H. M. *The Art of Block Building.* New York: Bank Street College of Education Publications, 1966 (first published in 1933).

Leeb-Lundberg, K. "Kindergarten Mathematics Laboratory." *The Arithmetic Teacher* 17, no. 5 (1970): 372–386.

Leeb-Lundberg, K. "Friedrich Froebel's Mathematics for the Kindergarten. Philosophy, Program and Implementation in the United Sates." Unpublished doctoral dissertation, New York University, 1972.

Lovell, K. *The Growth of Basic Mathematical and Scientific Concepts in Children.* London: University of London Press, 1964.

Lovell, K. *The Growth of Understanding in Mathematics: Kindergarten Through Grade Three.* New York: Holt, Rinehart & Winston, 1971.

Piaget, J. *The Child's Conception of Number.* New York: W. W. Norton, 1965.

Piaget, J., and Inhelder, B. *The Child's Conception of Space.* London: Routledge and Kegan Paul, 1967.

Piaget, J.; Inhelder, B.; and Szeminska, A. *The Child's Conception of Geometry.* New York: Harper & Row, 1964.

Pratt, C. *The Play School: An Experiment in Education.* Bureau of Educational Experiments. Bulletin No. 3. New York: Bank Street College of Education, 1917.

Pratt, C., and Stanton, J. *Before Books.* New York: Adelphi, 1926.

Wadsworth, B. J. *Piaget's Theory of Cognitive Development.* 2nd ed. New York: Longman, 1979.

Wright, F. L. *An Autobiography.* New York: Longman, Green, 1932.

Charlotte Brody

Social studies and self-awareness

A young child was asked what she learned in nursery school; "I learned to be," she replied. To be what? To be a member of a peer group. This is a big step forward when you consider that the child's world is an egocentric one. Before the age of two, almost all of a child's needs are fulfilled by others. Children's perception of people and their functions all radiate from themselves.

In the short time that children have lived, their home has been the environment in which they have had experiences. Now, at school, there is a new environment, new materials, new people with new functions, and new demands on children. One of these new materials is blocks. First buildings are usually blocks placed horizontally, one next to the other. They are generally of the same size. This configuration appears to be a road, a train, or a track to the adult. In children's fantasies, the block formation may be something entirely different. Children are not limited in their play by what they actually see. They are at what Piaget calls the preoperational stage. Fantasy and reality are not clearly differentiated. Piaget gives the example of a child of this age: "He is upset if someone tramps on a stone which he has designated as a turtle" (Elkind 1968, p. 62).

Young children know that they are using a concrete material, blocks, but their thoughts and imagination create wonderful, fanciful things. The simple structure described before may be a tunnel for cars and for people to children. They build a bridge and then drive cars under it. That a tunnel needs to have a roof because it is built under water or under a mountain is not important. The fact that a tunnel is built over water does not matter either, at this time. Clarification can come later. Now the children's imagination rules their behavior. There will be, at a later date, the separating out of fantasy and reality. Children need now to concretize their ideas, even though they are not necessarily recognizable to adults.

Teachers are often so convinced that they know what children mean to build that they verbalize their perceptions rather than asking questions of the children and allowing them to discuss and describe what they are building. Their reality is made up of their wishes, their feelings, and their thoughts. If given the opportunity, children will show the sequence of their thinking. Caroline Pratt and Jessie Stanton give an example of this in *Before Books*.

> A toy horse, returned to school by some one and left on the window seat, was instantly seen by Diana. I said she could have it when she made a stable for it. She and Elizabeth, a new child this year, both began to build. Elizabeth made a tiny construction but could not put the horse into it. It did not occur to her to change the size of the stable. Diana, on the other hand, having built a large stable with a low roof, after several attempts to force the horse in, removed the blocks composing the roof, made the walls higher, and replaced the roof. She then tried to put into words what she had done, saying, "Roof too small." I gave her the words "high" and "low", and she went about the room smiling and repeating the explanation to the other children. Diana added a room on top of the stable, and Matthew said, "You can keep the hay up there." (1926, pp. 30–31)

Adults must constantly be on the alert not to assume that words are knowledge. Some children verbalize early and do it smoothly, but, when the expressed ideas are put into another frame of reference, it becomes clear that the children are repeating adult words without comprehension. Young children who talk about a big building usually mean something that is taller than they are. Their sense of proportion and relationships are related to their size. In the example of the child who made a stable that was too small for the horse, the child was unable to see the relative size of the horse and the stable until she had actually put them together. The words to describe size relationships were new and not fully understood. Many differ-

Cooperation and acceptance of each other's input occurs when children have an atmosphere in which they can experiment.

ent experiences in connection with the verbalization are needed before words take on full meaning. Peller states:

> Let us go to the very simplest quality of play: The playing child repeats an experience he has had, or a part of it. Repeating it, he divests it of its uniqueness. . . . The young child meets "Unprecedents" all the time. He has only a limited ability to recapture an image by repeating its verbal label or by repeating it in thought. Play enables the child to re-experience, to remold past impressions and events and their accompanying moods and emotions. Playful repetition provides essential, possibly indispensable steps toward concept formation. (n.d.)

Early buildings are usually done in solitary splendor, and the accidental bumping of two bodies, both bent on their own building, may lead to the joining of the two. It may be as simple as connecting two sets of tracks, but this is the next step in socialization. The accidental associating with another child opens a new vista. Each child alone may have quickly lost interest in block building, but together they continue to build and to use the tracks. The addition of other ideas increases interest and often makes children more aware of what they are doing. An example from *Before Books:*

> Railroad tracks are becoming the dominant interest of the group, and more concentrated work is done in this occupation at present than in any other. There is much enjoyment in cooperation and, though building may begin alone, tracks are usually connected with each other. On Monday, Craig made the usual type of track, but Matthew placed unit blocks in an upright position beside the track. When Craig began to run a train near this part of the track, Matthew said, "That's the Subway, wait, it isn't finished yet, I'm going to make it dark." Then he started to lay blocks on top. The first size he tried was too short. He recognized this at once, went for a larger size, and put one on, when Craig interfered, saying, "That's not right, you must make it higher so cars can go in it." Matthew accepted this and they made the sides higher and added a roof. The other part of the track became a trolley track, and a large car barn was added. (Pratt and Stanton 1926, pp. 30–31)

This example of cooperation and acceptance of each other's input occurs when children have an atmosphere in which they can experiment. The re-creation of the child's world requires that the teacher be close enough to assist when it seems necessary. If Matthew had not been able to accept the fact that a larger size block was needed, the adult might have had to watch the situation to see what happened. Craig could see size relationships, but what if Matthew had tried smaller blocks and they did not work? He would have needed the opportunity to try and to fail, and then to try again so that he could succeed. The placing together of several blocks and using them as a track is a feat of accomplishment. *Look what I did,* children may say, not verbally, but in the way in which they look at the adult. Recognition of this success should be given, not necessarily verbally, but at least with a returned look of pleasure or a nod of approval. Children at the youngest age need to have a feeling of competence. White, who considers competence motivation a powerful driving force, gives the following definition:

> The concept of competence subsumes the whole realm of learned behavior whereby the child comes to deal effectively with his environment. It includes manipulation, locomotion, language, the building of cognitive maps and skilled actions, and the growth of effective behavior in relation to other people. These acquisitions are made by young animals and children partly through exploratory and manipulative play . . . The child's actual competence and his sense of competence [are] held to be a crucial element in any psychology of the ego. (1966, p. 307)

Caroline Pratt gives an example of how children view their work:

> They were indeed developing work habits. Their play with the blocks made this very clear. Building a railroad with blocks may look like play to an adult, but to the children it is work. There comes the moment when it is even drudgery, like building a structure over and over until it stands. The discipline of work is as surely present as it is in any adult creative venture. As a matter of fact, it was at about this time that we dropped the name Play School because the children resented it! (1948, p. 17)

Changes that occur in buildings, at an early stage, are made at the spur of the moment. A house may be just four walls, and then the thought occurs that a house needs a roof. The problem now is to determine what size block will span the building so that the roof will not cave in. The simplest roofs are flat, but at a later stage in development we see children having peaked roofs on their buildings.

The inability to delay gratification may make it necessary for some children to work alone. This need, to work alone, lasts for

Preplanning occurs when children can put their thoughts into words.

varying periods of time. For some children it is an escape from group pressures and for others it is the only time and place they can do what gives them pleasure. The retreat into fantasy cannot be shared with others. To verbalize might destroy the magic of the moment. The lack of planning does not interfere with the children's use of the building. They know what they are doing and are content.

The teacher's responsibility to help children grow must also extend to the growth that occurs through social interaction. The two children who accidentally join buildings make changes in each of their buildings based on the action of the other child. In *Before Books*, we see this example:

> The new feature in block building this week has been the fine cooperation displayed by children working together. Annie was the only child to build alone. When Mark began a track on Thursday, he said, "I want somebody to build with me," and Annie, putting away her own blocks, joined him. (Pratt and Stanton 1926, p. 97)

Here we see the moment when children seek others and no longer want to work alone. The need to socialize comes with growth. The ability to accept what another child suggests and not to rebel, even if things do not work out, is seen in this example:

Mark foresaw the size of the block needed for a certain space and said, "We need a small block." Then he ran to the cupboard and, bringing the block back, fitted it into the space while Murray jumped up and down with excitement. Mark then returned for more blocks and came back with four, saying, "I'm taking four blocks." Murray did the same, only he said, "I'm taking three blocks," which was correct. The house being finished now, they ran to the cupboard for the fire engine. Each wanted an engine, but there was only one, so I suggested they use another kind of wagon as an engine. This turned out to be impractical, as each child who had made a wagon recognized his or hers as it came from the shelves, and called out that it was a milk wagon, or a lumber wagon. Mark and Murray then made efforts to adjust to the situation of only one engine. Mark said to Murray, who was holding it, "Would you just lend me your fire engine?" And then they said something about turns and carried it over and put it in the house. (Pratt and Stanton 1926, p. 97)

This cooperative venture did not end when there was only one fire engine. The ability of the children to see the taking of turns as a solution to a problem is growth.

Preplanning occurs at a time when children can put their thoughts into words. Children communicate ideas. They can verbalize the fact that a road needs grading so that cars can ride smoothly from the floor onto the road and can leave the road in the same smooth manner. How to bridge the space from floor to road? A ramp! This is the way that real cars drive safely and smoothly from one plane to another.

The need for greater realism is evidenced by the use of auxiliary materials. Signs, people, animals, as well as vehicles, are needed when building and using a road. Signs help people to know when to stop and where to stop. Signs tell people where they are and where they are going. Signs tell you the number of the road. Signs tell you how fast you may drive. Signs tell you where you can get on the road and where you can get off. Signs tell where you can eat and where you can purchase gasoline. Signs dot the landscape of the real road and, therefore, need to be a part of a child's road. In my own experience, I have never seen chilidren make road signs to advertise commercial products, thank goodness; nevertheless, they, too, are a part of the child's real world. These additions are helping children to enlarge their awareness of the world around them.

All the signs are indications that there are people in different places doing different things. *Who are these people and what do they do? Who put up the signs? Who made the signs? Why are the signs needed?* Adult questioning of why a sign is needed that says STOP may elicit a concern that somebody has to stop so that the cars won't have an accident. If you need gasoline, you need to know where you can buy it. *Who sells the gasoline and what kind of a building do you need?* Children can be helped to consider further the many people necessary for the automobile to function. If you build a garage, it has to have a gas pump and a person to pump the gas. *What if the car does not go?* The garage has to have a place and a person to service it—a mechanic.

There is a vocabulary for each of these occupations and there are special tools needed. In *Young Geographers,* Mitchell describes this learning through relationships.

> The modern school asserts that children grow in mental maturity from the very beginning by the active process of discovering relationships and regards the school essentially as a laboratory where such discoveries may be made. Children are born in the world full of discrete sensations, experiences, and at once begin the marvelous process of relating these experiences, one to another. The learning process is essentially the same, literally from the cradle to the grave. But the facts and ideas to be related grow in complexity as they are built on wider and wider experiences and more elaborated ideas. (1971 [1921], p. 11)

The community of people working together in the school helps children to understand the interdependence of people. Kindergarten age children are ready for this wider view of the world around them. Mitchell goes on:

> The first facts to be related are those in the children's immediate environment: The tools by which they discover the relationships are their own sense and motor experiences. The method is that of the laboratory: experimentation. These answers involve the school immediately in a study of the environment (which is all the surrounding influences including regional geography for children old enough to take trips) and lead to a development of a pedagogy and a curriculum in which geography, in the new sense, bulks large. The practical tasks for each school are to study the geographic relations in the environment into which their children are born and to watch the children's behavior in their environment, to note when they first discover relations, and what they are. On the basis of these findings each school will make its own curriculum for small children. To base a curriculum for small children upon a study of their environment seems at first glance

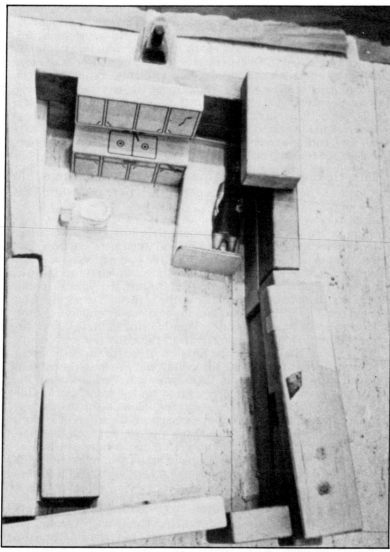

Scale is not important at this time, but there is the awareness of the ability to represent places in another way and with a concrete three-dimensional material. This is the beginning of map making.

preposterous. For modern children are born into an appallingly complicated world. A three-year-old in a city environment may be whisked to his steam-heated nursery in an electric elevator, fed from supplies which are ordered by telephone, sent up in a dumb-waiter and stored in an electric refrigerator; he may be taken to a hole in the sidewalk and borne rapidly on an underground train to a distant place. The forces which move his elevator, warm his nursery, extend his mother's voice to a grocery store, cool his milk, propel the subway train, are complicated and difficult to understand not only at three, at six, but even at forty. He lives in a world of end-products with the functioning causes largely concealed (1971[1921], p. 11)

With children's increased awareness of relationships, they can look at the school and its personnel. In *Our Children and Our Schools*, Mitchell describes the trips:

So our trips with kindergarteners were to see how work was done—work that was closely tied up with their personal lives. The trips had to be near by, for these children had not been on group trips and had no idea of the kind of behavior which is necessary in a group for safety. The first trips were within the school—to talk with the school nurse; to talk with the principal; to see the food being cooked for the lunchroom; to see the older children getting ready the milk bottles they were later to bring to these kindergarten children; to see the pile of coal in the cellar and custodian's helper shovel the coal into the furnace; to see the pipes that went from the furnace and along the ceiling and finally appeared connected with the radiators in their own room. Perhaps to see the coal truck and watch the driver grind up the truck, put up the chute, take the cover off the hole in the sidewalk, and let the coal rattle down to the school cellar. Perhaps a walk around the block to see what they could see. Perhaps a pause to watch the shoemaker putting new soles on shoes, or the laundryman ironing clothes, or the man with the grindstone sharpening scissors and knives, or the grocer selling vegetables, fruit and other groceries. (1951, p. 133)

These special places can then be re-created in the block corner. One can build the kindergarten room with blocks, then the lunchroom. *Where is the lunchroom in relation to the classroom? Where are the bathrooms? Where is the front door? Where is the outdoor play area?* Five-year-olds are able to plan their buildings in small groups of two, three, five, or more. Mary and John are making the classroom and Jimmy places the kitchen right next to it. A chorus of "No, that's the wrong place" corrects Jimmy. "The kitchen is down the hall."

Now there is a conference of several children who have been drawn to the blocks to assist the three who are building. They all become involved in a discussion of where to place the kitchen and how to build the hallway that you have to walk down before you can get to the kitchen. *Is that a kitchen? How do you know?* Just to say that this is the kitchen and that is the classroom is not enough. You have to have things in the rooms that show what they are. *What is in the classroom?* Chairs, tables, shelves, a piano, people—some of these are available in the box that has accessories to use with the block buildings and some things have to be made.

What is in a kitchen? Stove, refrigerator, sink, table, chairs, garbage can, work space, other cooking equipment? How much of this is discussed by the children would depend on their maturity and ability, but the important thing is that they are aware of the way in which rooms are identified. A sign saying *kitchen* or *classroom* could be an identification, but that is not the way that children identify. They know what something is by the concrete things that they see. They do not read the written signs. They read the name of the room by the unwritten symbols, the things that are identifiable—their use. The need for a sign should come from the children to the adult. Teachers must be careful not to put their ideas into the discussion before the children are ready for them. Teacher sensitivity is most important.

What of the discussion of where to place the rooms in relation to each other? What of the idea of building the classroom with blocks? Why? This is the beginning of map making. The block building is smaller in scale but does represent the whole room. Scale is not important at this time, but there is the awareness of the ability to represent places in another way and with a concrete three-dimensional material. The actual making of maps on paper comes at a later stage in development, but the initial exposure has been made with the blocks.

Starks cites the reverse situation, when creative block building leads to a trip.

Carol, a rather mature five-year-old who rarely used blocks, began working one day on a tall building. The center part of one end was hollow and the other end had four floor levels. Soon she asked for string and proceeded to cut several pieces which she tied to a block. This she dropped into the open well of the building. By that time Jake and several other children had gathered around to see what she was doing. "It's an elevator," Carol announced happily. "See the people are going up to the roof restaurant for lunch." She had trouble pulling the block up and down, however, and many suggestions were contributed by the interested spectators. With frank admiration, Tony (who was usually the instigator of elaborate ideas) announced, "I'll help you Carol. I'll help you work it so that the people won't fall off." Interest in the elevator and its working and use led to a trip for part of the group to one of the older buildings in town where the cables and elevator could be watched through an open grille. Comments heard during the trip were put to use upon returning to the school: "It's a big cage with a building around it." "Big steel cables pull it up. There's a wheel—a pulley—that winds the cables and lifts the elevator." "You tell the man (operator) what floor you want and he stops the elevator at that floor. He makes the pulley stop winding the cable and that stops it." "An elevator is a cage you ride up in. An escalator is stair steps that move." As a result of the trip, a small box was used as the elevator. Strings at each end led to the roof where they were wound around a cylinder and could be rolled up or down as desired. Carol, her idea, and her construction became the center of a group varying in size from four to twelve during the period of at least two weeks. During the remainder of the year others experimented with the idea with varying degrees of success. (1970)

Structures at five are more complex; there is a greater awareness of balance, more intricate use of blocks. Curves, arches, cylinders, and triangles are used as part of the building or as decorations or ornamentation on buildings. Functionalism is the only criterion. The awareness that there can be substitutions of sizes aids children in group living by making it possible for them to go on with their building although all the blocks of the size that they wanted are in use.

The block buildings of five-year-olds require more space than does the work of younger children. These more detailed buildings usually require more time to build and may need more than one session to build and to use. Letting buildings stay up overnight, and possibly for several days, increases the value to children. It might take all the allotted time to build the swimming pool, to color a paper to indicate the water, to construct a diving board, and to put people in and around it. *Where is the time to use it? Where is the time to involve others in the building? Where is the time to tell others about the building?* Children need to have time to dramatize and to include other members of the group in this activity. The cooperation that went into the construction of the building, the pride in the construction, are just part of the whole. The need to use the building is as great as the need to make it. Teachers have to be aware of this when they plan the time and the space for their block corners.

Antin describing the block play of six-year-olds says:

> Block play lends itself particularly to developmental work in the early school years. It offers opportunity for group focus, yet allows for related play on various levels. It is one of the natural materials for children, giving them great satisfaction and fun. It feeds vigorously and directly into academic studies, using social studies as a center of interest. But, why block work at six? At about six years it becomes important to try to function apart from the family. The strong push from within is to belong to a group of one's own choosing—to fashion oneself as a member of that group. This period of self-discovery, of unsureness of one's abilities and strengths, must of necessity result, at times, in awkward behavior. (1952, p. 2)

She then goes on to describe the further development of the social studies program of the six-year-olds.

> An exciting study of food coming into our city by trains and barges, over bridges and through tunnels, also includes activities which answer the needs of children who are still playing out home and family relationships. For who ever heard of a city where there are no houses for people to live in? Where do the boat and train-men go at the end of the day's work? How can people live without department stores? Or grocery stores, jewelry shops, restaurants, garages, banks, playgrounds, beauty parlors? Buses are needed and sight-seeing boats. The block-city needs people, and people properly dressed. Plasticine comes to the rescue, and bits of material, paper, crayons, scissors and paste. Docks and trains need number signs. Buildings, streets, boats, businesses have names. Traffic signs and danger signals are needed. Money, with the number quantity written on it, becomes necessary. What goes on here? John's railroad tracks are crowding out streets for taxis and trucks! And freight coming into our city must be shipped from all over the country by train. When we were down by the markets how did we see our city work it out? Hundreds of trucks and cars fill the streets and yet the trains came in and went out! An over-pass is needed! 'Detour. Over-pass being built.' And so it goes." (1952, p. 2)

Now, at six, children are ready for and need the written

In social studies, we deal with people and their relationships to each other through time and space. Children need the time and the space to experience, to learn, and to grow.

signs. These are important because of the complexity of the block buildings. The larger geographic unit called a city requires greater awareness of how people live and work together. This re-creation of trips helps children to orient themselves directionally so that they can then take this knowledge back to the classroom.

Caroline Pratt describes just such an occurrence in *Before Books:*

> The blocks have come into their own this week. The children have used them with keen interest, and have made play schemes which have been enlarged from day to day. All but three children in the class have taken part in them and other activities have been related to their block play. On Monday, I asked Fred what he was going to build when he returned to class and he replied: "Wanamaker's." Meta said she would make "Seventh Avenue" and Florence decided to build her apartment house on Washington Square. Ready to work in the room, I asked Fred where he thought he had better make Wanamaker's and chose correctly the east side of the room. Meta made Seventh Avenue with blocks on the west

side. She left spaces for the cross streets and drew them with chalk from Fourth to Twelfth Street. She had a very clear conception of the way the streets ran. She built her apartment house on Fourth Street. I showed Florence where Seventh Avenue and Eighth Street were, and she built her apartment on the next street to the south. A large round cylinder block placed in a square, puzzled me, but Florence informed me that it was the boiler in the cellar, and held the hot water that heated the building. She made Washington Square next. Dolls were seated on benches. Paper scratched over with green crayon represented the grass. Sonia made the Woolworth Tower at the extreme south end of the room. Fred worked steadily on Wanamaker's. The only things within the very large square which represented the store were the elevator and some "offices." It is interesting to note that what Fred has seen chiefly in watching the elevator was the great rod that pushed it up. He represented this by a very long block, which he stood upright. Thumb-tacks on blocks represented the elevator lights which he had watched. He made the door by which we had entered in exactly the correct location, the south east corner, and drew marks on the floor to represent our class going in. Celia built the school and Alan his own house.

Sonia wanted to play with the toy horse, so she made a stable at the foot of the Woolworth Tower. I find that my tendency is to insist on too great accuracy from these six-year-olds. On this occasion I merely remarked that of course the Woolworth didn't really have horses in it, which Sonia knew, and a very good play developed later with Edna, who made a blacksmith shop nearby, when Sonia demanded new shoes for her animals. (Pratt and Stanton 1926, p. 15)

Older children are ready for greater representation and appear to be more specific in their buildings. Hirsch discussing representation says:

The acquisition of representational knowledge has long been part and parcel of good early childhood programs. The unit blocks originally designed by Caroline Pratt in the "progressive-school" era of the thirties and described by Lucy Sprague Mitchell in *Young Geographers* are still excellent tools for understanding spatial relationships. In the film *Incitement to Reading* a combined class of first and second graders explores their environment and reproduces it by using blocks. The film shows with clarity spatial and directional confusions and their resolution through the use of blocks. This is the beginning of mapmaking, through the manipulation of three-dimensional objects in order to represent spatial arrangements. There is another scene in this film that illustrates the use of blocks in the study of social problems. Children who obviously have never seen a large city tackle the problem of limited space for many people and arrive at a solution through their block building: buildings will have to be higher! (1974, pp. 47–49)

The block work that helps children in their discovery of their environment makes many demands on them. They have to communicate, exchange ideas, plan, and execute. After the building is finished, there is need for further communication, further exchange of ideas and perhaps a change in the building plans. The ability to preplan, to cooperate, to give, and to take extends beyond the block area. It becomes part of children. They learn to think clearly and to express themselves clearly. They learn to discipline themselves in order to be a contributing member of their peer group. They learn to discipline themselves in order to concentrate. They are learning about group functioning. All of this becomes part of children on the way to becoming adults.

The time table of growth from the dependent infant to the independent school age child is as individual and different as they are. Children need assistance and encouragement, at home and at school, in their attempts at ever greater independence. They need to have time to learn about themselves and their abilities. They need to have an ever large environment for new experiences. These experiences are only meaningful if the children can relate them to something they already know and have experienced. The sequence from the known (previous experience) to the unknown (new experience) is not always easy and comfortable for young children. As they mature and become more aware of themselves, they realize that the unknown can be tried with greater ease and that there is a pleasure in new experiences, new conquests. The relationships with other people, children, and adults is the basis of social studies. In social studies, we deal with people and their relationships to each other through time and space. Children need the time and the space to experience, to learn, and to grow.

References

Antin, C. *Blocks in the Curriculum.* New York: Early Childhood Education Council of New York City, 1952.

Elkind, D. "An Influence as Great as Freud: Jean Piaget." *The New York Times Magazine* (May 26, 1968): 62.

Hirsch, E. S. "Reaction II." (Response to Bernard Spodek's "Social Studies for Young Children: Identifying Intellectual Goals.") *Social Education* 38, no. 1 (1974): 47–49.

Mitchell, L. S. *Our Children and Our Schools.* New York: Simon & Schuster, 1951.

Mitchell, L. S. *Young Geographers.* New York: John Day, 1921; New York: Agathon Press, 1971.

Peller, L. "Models of Children's Play." Paper presented at The City College of New York, n. d.

Pratt, C. *I Learn from Children.* New York: Simon & Schuster, 1948.

Pratt C., and Stanton, J. *Before Books.* New York: Adelphi, 1926.

Starks, E. B. *Blockbuilding.* Washington, D.C.: American Association of Elementary-Kindergarten-Nursery Educators, 1970.

White, R. W. "Competence and the Psychosexual Stages of Development." In *The Causes of Behavior,* ed. J. F. Rosenblith and W. Allinsmith. Boston: Allyn & Bacon, 1966.

Harriet K. Cuffaro

Dramatic play
The experience of block building

One of the most profound means available to children for constructing and reconstructing, formulating and reformulating knowledge is through play. It is a means for synthesis and integration in that it brings together the child's concept of reality with the inner world of fantasies and feelings. Play may be seen as the child's substitute for adult musing, contemplation, hypothesizing, meandering among ideas, and experiences. Play is the visible language of childhood wherein we see and hear the total child functioning, revealing individual concerns, conflicts, information and misinformation, ambivalences, wishes, hopes, pleasures, and questions. Where the adult discusses an experience and via words—thought or spoken—explores nuances, connections, and possible meanings, the child requires the context of activity for such probing and exploration. Isaacs states:

> Verbal thinking can hardly yet be *sustained in its own right*, in earlier years. It draws its vitality from the actual problems of concrete understanding and of manipulation in which it takes its rise and solution of which it furthers. (1966, pp. 84–85)

Play encompasses an almost infinite variety of activities. The growing literature on play, aside from exploring its variety and meaning, has also indicated how difficult it is to capture this activity of childhood in definition. What follows is not a definition of play, but rather a statement of elements which I deem necessary to its consideration.

Two things seem to be essential—activity and self-direction.

Activity here is defined not only as motion, as in walking, running, reaching, but also the activity, the engagement, of the senses. Self-direction explains itself; the direction of the activity is determined by the child. What starts play, how it proceeds, where it leads, when it stops, what it includes or excludes, what it ignores or connects to—these are choices made by the child consciously or unconsciously. Many factors influence the child's selection. Important among them is the level of development which determines functioning ability; the degree of interest, curiosity, and knowledge invested, the individual's use of affect—that uniquely personal conglomerate of feelings and fantasies born of interaction with the world of people and things.

There are many kinds of play which include these two elements. The chapter headings in Lowenfeld's *Play in Childhood* (1967, Table of Contents) reveal not only an interesting classification of play activities, but also the varying functions of play. For example: "play as bodily activity; play as repetition of experience; play as the demonstration of fantasy; play as realization of environment; play as preparation for life." In other writers may be found phrases such as imaginative play and imitative play. My focus is on yet another label for play—one which includes aspects of all the classifications stated above—*dramatic play.*

The word drama evokes visions of theater. The child's dramatic play and the world of theater may find alliance and provoke comparison. Both deal with a blending of reality, fantasy, and imagination unpressured by time and space—elements which are used personally and uniquely. In each, a world is selectively created from aspects of reality and with feelings and wishes blended through imagination to reflect a particular view, a personal understanding. To carry the analogy further, in dramatic play the script is created out of the child's totality of experience; the cast is the child performing as self and also as other selves reflecting roles being imitated, rehearsed, or projected. Dramatic play is a play always in rehearsal, an ongoing production. What is understood, explored, initiated, reconstructed, synthesized moves into the script, thereby altering it while in production.

Dramatic play may occur in many settings, engaging a child

The general setting for dramatic play is created by the adult in the allocation of space, the number and variety of blocks provided, and the addition of supplementary materials such as people and animals, cars, planes, and boats.

alone or with others, with or without props. We see it in the child sitting alone driving a bus; in a group of children sitting in a school yard on a picnic in the park; in a serious little group engrossed in the drama of a sick baby attended by a doctor; two children involved in a primeval battle between two clay dinosaurs they have molded, in the busy activity of a child collecting garbage on a truck from house to house in a city block scheme. Each of the situations mentioned has its own possibilities, defined by the limitations and potential of the particular medium being used, by the setting, and by the child.

In narrowing the focus of investigation to the dramatic play which may occur in relation to block building in a *group setting*, it would be helpful to explore not only the play of the child but also the nature of the medium and how it affects and influences activity.

Throughout this chapter, the blocks referred to are the blocks for indoor use designed by Caroline Pratt. They do not bear her name but are sold under various trademarks. When reference is made to the larger hollow blocks, it will be so specified.

Block building and dramatic play

I would broadly define dramatic play with blocks as the self-directed activity which occurs between a child and the structure created by the child and wherein a transactional relationship exists between subject and object. The child creates an object—the structure—and endows it in imagination with representations and reflections of her or his experiences, fantasies, information. The structure is then a tangible representation to the child of personal ideas and feelings, and, in this symbolic form, then serves as a stimulus for expanding activity and imaginings. It becomes, for the child, a tangible point of reference for questioning and contemplation, activities which would be difficult without connection with the concrete. As the child explores reality and as ideas are expanded, this flow of thoughts and feelings is reflected in the changes the child makes in the structure. For example, amendments to a building, alterations, and details, may be seen as the child's record-

ing the development of an idea. This recording then may serve as a means for review and further examination when the structure is used.

Just as building structures may follow a developmental progression, vividly and richly documented by Harriet Johnson's *The Art of Block Building,* so does the play connected with it. Generally, it seems to move in stages from solitary play in which there are brief encounters with others, to play of a more associative nature in which one or two children will work loosely connected to other clusters, to play which is in cooperation with others and which is more sustained, often planned, and extends over a longer period of time.

No matter in which of the above stages the child might be, using blocks for dramatic play requires the child to: (1) create the context for play rather than finding it; (2) deal with reality and scale in translating ideas to the medium; (3) gradually step outside of self to a symbolized self in play. These three tasks will be discussed in greater detail. It is usually in the cooperative play of five-year-olds, especially those who have had the opportunity to use blocks freely and with sufficient time to explore ideas, that many of these characteristics will appear most clearly. By this age, the child's experiences in the social and physical world have helped to expand perspective and knowledge. By five children's horizons have been extended beyond the immediacy of family, and they are ready to exercise this understanding. (While mentioning a specific age, I simultaneously add the caution that such usage is an approximation because many factors—culture, experience, development, maturation, socioeconomic setting, etc.—influence chronology. It should also be considered that children function on various levels of development, incorporating into the present moment elements of the past while also stretching toward the future.)

Creating the context for play

The general setting for dramatic play is created by the adult in the allocation of space, the number and variety of blocks provided, and the addition of supplementary materials such as rubber/wooden people and animals, cars, planes, boats, cloth, paper, string, colored cubes, containers, and sticks. The space

The house may represent the conglomerate of houses known; it may be a selection of images from those features which have the most meaning for the child.

should be adequate and not hampered by being a passageway for traffic or encumbered by tables and other furniture.

In a sense, a theater with bare stage has been made ready with props available for creating the set. In a housekeeping area, the child *finds* the set of refrigerator, stove, sink, bed, table, chairs, etc. In the block area, the child must *create* the set of context for the play that will unfold. In the former instance, the child enacts a role in a setting established by others; in the latter, the child not only enacts a role, but is also called upon to design and produce the setting. Blocks do not make a statement in themselves other than conveying a feeling of harmony and durability. This is in contrast to a stove or sink in the housekeeping area which is clearly defined. Of course, the child is free to imagine the stove to be a boat by ignoring its detail. In such an instance, it would seem that the child is not engaged with the stove itself; it becomes merely a stepping stone for the flow of ideas. Building the child's own stove, through the realization of an idea in tangible form, is an act of creation.

The block, in having no predetermined identity other than its physical state of smoothness, hardness, and shape, is a blank on which or with which children make their impact. Children must *do* and *make* in order for play to commence. The younger the child, the greater is the emphasis on the *doing* and self-participation. Later, the *making, creating,* is added to action. For example, a young three-year-old may take a block and push it across the floor, tooting, puffing, swaying as a boat. Child, block, boat are fused into a oneness that is generalized, global. In this younger stage, it is the *feel* of the boat— the being-imagining of boatness—that is externalized in physical expression. As play evolves, the details of reality and information are added, and some separation begins to occur between self and object. It is no longer sufficient to endow the object through sound and motion and to imagine that it is a boat. It has to take form and must be physically endowed as a boat. Size and shape of blocks take on a new importance as the child moves to grouping, selecting, and arranging blocks to create the boat. Some of that earlier *feel* is now *out* of self and passed onto the details of the object.

Reality and scale in translation of idea to medium

No matter how a structure is started—whether a child comes to the block shelf ready to build a house or whether the structure becomes a house as blocks are handled—the child's task is to translate an idea into actuality. The house may represent the conglomerate of houses known; it may be a selection of images from those features which have the most meaning for the child. The representation will include the child's information about houses and the child's feelings about them. It may be a house consisting solely of a kitchen, or one with rooms for people and animals, or a barricaded building without windows or doors. Whatever it becomes, the task of the child is to translate an idea/concept which is internalized into an externalized representation. In the translation of images, the child must deal structurally with the question of relationships—balance, fit, proportion, order, etc. In the act of symbolizing, the child is assisted by the unitary, harmonious nature of blocks. In their scaled order, blocks promote proportion and relationships which may support the child's task of connecting fragments of images and feelings toward a combined whole, a synthesis. Also, the fact that blocks cannot be altered, bent, or folded, requires that the child adapt to the demands of that reality.

The unyielding, durable nature of the material and its characteristics of harmony and scale are part of the world of reality, and it is into that real world that children seek to bring their images. I recall the dilemma of a child working out a turn on his two-way elevated highway. He was distressed by the lack of smoothness in his incline and the turn itself. These were some of his thoughts as he accompanied action with words: "If you have a bump when you turn you could have an accident; if I don't turn here my highway can't go anywhere, only into that building and a highway doesn't go *into* buildings; that kind of block doesn't fit, it's too big for the way my highway grows; it has to be bigger here (width) when it goes around 'cause how will the other car (coming from opposite direction) know where its place is to be safe." He finally worked it out by driving a car back and forth, looking, trying, changing blocks, and in a triumphant moment, when all the trying jelled: "Wait, wait. I know!" He altered the incline of the ramp leading to the curve, and everything literally fell into place. Process and product were intertwined as the child evoked from self the representation to be created.

Distancing: from self to symbolic self and other symbolizations

In the process of distancing, the child separates from self that which is within the self. As mentioned earlier, when the very young child is exploring a boat, it may be done with any object that can be moved. In such doing, there is a flow between child and object as they mesh together. Gradually, and over an extended period of time and experiences, the child moves in dramatic play to a more objective directing of objects and props which support the play. A series of examples may serve to illustrate this evolution.

1. A young four-year-old builds a simple block structure called a house and plays the role of mother to a baby doll. Another child joins the play and becomes the pet kitten. Yet another child joins the group and becomes the big brother. Although the group has enlarged, the structure may remain

the same. Possibly an enclosure may be added to house the four-year-old curled into a ball and meowing. If needed, the other children may stretch out on the floor near the building.

2. With the same group toward the end of the year, we may find the same child once again building a house. Now the house may be more complex with partitions creating rooms rather than the previous suggestion of a room. On the bed, we again find the doll and next to it the big brother who this time is not a child, but a rubber/wooden figure. The kitten, still meowing and purring, lies in a more elaborate environment: bowl for milk, pillow, and blanket, a decoration for play.

3. And yet another example, as our small group is now five-year-olds in the spring of the following year. I recall a specific house complete with kitchen, bedrooms, living room, and many bathrooms. Each of the rooms was furnished in great detail. Small drawings were pasted on the walls as framed pictures. The kitchen's stove, refrigerator, sink, built of unit blocks and squares, had paper taped on them indicating the jets, faucets, and door knobs. In the house lived a family of rubber people—mother, father, two sisters, and a baby brother.

These three examples illustrate some progressive stages in the development of dramatic play with blocks: increasing attention given to the details of reality and the question of scale, which were discussed in the preceding section; gradual movement from involvement in play via direct participation to participation through a symbolized self represented by a rubber/wooden figure, which will now be explored.

A lessening of egocentricity is one of the necessary steps in cognitive development which sees as a goal the ability to think logically, analytically, and objectively. Objectivity requires distance from self and the ability to comprehend frames of reference other than one's own. This cannot occur without the existence of opportunities, which reveal alternatives, or the feeling of discordance or conflict which may grow out of situations in which basic premises are shaken. Whenever a child takes yet another step in linking to the world of reality, such situations and opportunities become available. They are also present in the dramatic play accompanying block building, because children in play are re-creating their experiences and questions of the moment. As reality sharpens and takes more distinct form, it becomes more tangible. It separates from the global and thus the child is better able to examine, experiment with, and begin to direct that which has been differentiated. The role played may take on shading and variation. It would seem that as form becomes more definite, it also grows in depth as it is reinforced and rooted with the addition of detail and by conforming to the proportions and relationships found in reality.

The child begins a similar process in defining self in relation to the social world. In the three examples given in this section, we see how the structure of dramatic play may supply the child with situations and opportunities in which to examine and rehearse the processes of differentiation and individuation and their results. The child's *direct participation* through *self* in the first and second examples is relinquished in the third example to a symbolized self onto whom feelings and actions are *projected*. The child may stand outside of self for limited periods of time and function as if someone else, and enact a role in adherence to her or his understanding of this other role. In the projection onto a symbolized self/selves, the child is able to assume a *variety* of roles in rehearsal and imitation, to experiment with them without the pressure of time or consequences. Just as the child's knowledge of physical reality moves from the global to the specific and the child is thus able to examine, experiment with, and direct that which has taken form, so it is in the realm of people and feelings. Through play, the child has an opportunity to externalize a variety of emotions—amorphous, potent, ambivalent—and thus make them available for examination and understanding. Also externalized is the child's understanding of relationships and roles, knowledge which may be difficult to accept because it conflicts with wishes and desires, is confusing, or simply incomprehensible. In play, the child takes information and misinformation and tests it against reality. According to Isaacs:

> Play is not only the means by which the child comes to discover the world; it is supremely the activity which brings him psychic equilibrium in the early years. In his play activities, the child externalizes and works out to some measure of harmony all the different trends of his internal psychic life. . . . And gradually he learns to relate his deepest and most primitive phantasies to the ordered world of real relations. (1972, p. 425)

As some of the above remarks may be related to dramatic play generally, I would like to stress an essential difference that exists when the dramatic play is connected to block building. Once the child moves into using a symbolic self, i.e., the rubber/wooden figures, it becomes possible for the child to experiment with more roles. For example, a child in directing the activities of four rubber/wooden figures in a setting she or he has created may alternately be mother, baby, father, teacher. Not only is each role tested, but also the relationships existing among the various roles.

Finally, the process of building is in itself an act of distancing as the child externalizes thoughts and feelings. There are times when in the externalization the child creates a structure which is representative, but there are also times when the child engages in building activities which are exploratory and not necessarily goal directed. If our attention is caught only by the recognizable, then we may miss the steps leading to it. The seemingly aimless building in which a child may engage is an important step in the total process of symbolization. The importance of this step may be understood if we compare it to the time needed to fool around, to toy with an idea before it begins to take shape and find direction. There are many steps to be taken as the child externalizes thoughts and feelings. As Lowenfeld says,

> Play is in a sense artistic creation; each piece of play of this kind is a new creation, and its creation is intimately connected with the development of thought, for until a concept has been expressed, or an experience externalized, it cannot give place to another thought. (1967, p. 161)

Group setting

One further element to be considered in relation to this material is that block building and its accompanying dramatic play occur in a group setting. This fact has important implications, not only for the social development of the child, but also for cognitive and emotional development. A child working alone with blocks at home is still bringing to the building situation the elements mentioned earlier creating context for play, dealing with reality and scale in the translation of ideas,

Blocks permit children choices in the social context: you may build alone and ignore others; you may build alone and work with others; you may be part of a small group within a larger group; you may all accept a common challenge.

moving to a symbolized self in play. What ultimately would be missing if building were to continue as solitary play would be the impact and enrichment, the testing of one's knowledge and feelings, that may occur in interaction with the reality and feelings of others.

In the preceding section, three examples were given which illustrated the development of play around the central theme of *home* and certain progressions were noted. In examining the social aspects of this play, it should not be misunderstood that in such progressions, the number of children working together diminishes as surrogate figures take their place. On the contrary, social interaction is increased and expanded, as such play begins to take on a community aspect. From focus existing primarily in the complete world you have created, as in the first example of a self-sufficient group giving their attention to each other, we go to the last example where, from the established base of her home, the child could move out to all the possibilities offered by other children. For instance, in the last of the three illustrations, also to be found in the same block scheme were: a *school* (which her children attended); a *supermarket* (where she purchased her groceries which were usually milk, bread, ice cream, and candy); a *fire department* (workers came to put out a fire in her house which she refused to have, and so they went to another more obliging home); a *playground* (used by the school and to which she took her children, who were either very compliant or extraordinarily disobedient and accordingly rewarded or punished); a *hospital* (which she visited once because her baby had "a boiling fever"); a *department of sanitation* (she did not visit the incinerator plant, but dutifully complies with the directions of the garbage collectors); a *police station* (her only contact with the police was to thank them for returning her lost children).

Certain things become apparent in the brief parenthetical remarks concerning the nature of this child's interaction with the other children. Each child in that block scheme had created not only a structure, but also a set of rules which governed behavior and was appropriate to the role being played. In each encounter, she had to deal not only with her rules, but also with the rules of others, and there were instances when she found encounters with these other realities difficult to accept.

In addition, she was able to observe styles of functioning which differed from her own. She observed other interpretations of parental roles as other mothers and fathers took their children to the park and school. Of great importance was that she could regulate the degree of her participation. Without undue pressure, she could select those realities with which she could contend. She could engage in a variety of activities using the variety of identities within herself by directing the behavior of mother, father, baby, and other surrogate figures in her symbolic family.

Blocks permit children choices in the social context: you may build alone and ignore others; you may build alone and work with others; you may be part of a small group within a larger group; you may all accept a common challenge to work on. The variations are many. The material accommodates not only the sequence of social development, but also the moods and needs of the moment.

Educational Implications

This second part concerns itself with the application of the ideas presented. Formulas and activities will not be offered. Teachers must find the practices which are compatible with their values and which seem appropriate for the children with whom they are working. What will be presented are some underlying criteria for consideration on the part of teachers and a clearer definition of the opportunities offered.

Symbolization

It is a long road from cooing and babbling to speaking in coherent sentences, from an unplanned line on paper to the intentional writing of a word that can be read and understood. There are many steps to be taken on these roads, many pauses, detours. The child needs time to try and test skills and opportunities in which to use symbols in self-directed activities in order to get the *feel* of the process. The child must have the

As activity occurs in a group, the child is moved toward using and developing signs which may be understood by others.

chance to function on an *as if* level, to understand that one thing may stand for another. Dramatic play stemming from block building is a situation in which the child's symbolic activities grow out of the core of the child's living and consequently are relevant and meaningful to the child. In the externalization of images and feelings, both in actual building and in dramatic play, the child is engaged actively, functioning as an integrated self using body, feelings, senses, and thought. Within such opportunities children work themselves into the symbolic process with interest and a self-regulated tempo. In the doing, the child not only learns how to do, but also prepares for what will ultimately lead to the ability to work with abstract ideas, letters, numbers.

As children move into sign level representations, that is, into the realm of letters and numbers, punctuation marks, and mathematical notations, they need the time and the opportunities for experimentation and testing. Once again, children must get the *feel* of the process and begin to understand an order which they have not created, but must accept. Often, children may find entrance into this level of representation by giving birth to their own system; but, for such a system to be born, a need to communicate must exist. Such openings occur naturally in block building; scribbles on a piece of paper pasted on a road to indicate **warning;** arrows giving directions; colored cubes indicating traffic lights; a drawing of a flower to indicate a florist's shop; colored designs taped on a block house to indicate the address. From these beginnings grows the understanding which leads to the labels seen so frequently in block schemes: **STOP, danger, gas station, go slow, don't knock my building down, etc.** These messages dictated to teachers, often copied laboriously by children, are part of the experimentation begun in the simple scribbles drawn in imitation of the codes of the adult world.

The need for these symbols grows out of the activities of the child, thus imbuing them with personal meaning and significance. At first these personal symbols may have meaning only for the child, but as activity occurs in a group context, the child is moved toward using and developing signs which may be understood by others. This may also be extended to the communication involved in discussions and conversations which grow out of the happenings in a block scheme. Children have an opportunity to move from an egocentric to a sociocentric perspective as they exchange ideas, solve problems jointly, pose questions for each other, and begin to see how the world looks from the vantage point of another. In all these activities, their structures become a concrete base to which they may return for reference. Obviously, there are many opportunities offered in block building and dramatic play to create, use, and function within the symbolic realm. Such activities, growing out of the interests of the child, are an important phase in the development and refinement of the symbolic process.

Before proceeding to the next section, I would like to consider one further point in relation to the child's distancing through a symbolized self. As in other areas of development, when a child moves into a new stage, it does not mean that arrival signals new behavior which makes a clean break with the old. There is unevenness in behavior, a turning back at times to earlier modes of response. This becomes evident in dramatic play with blocks. For example, children who are perfectly able to use surrogate figures to represent self/selves in play with satisfaction and concentration may still need and use opportunities for more direct participation with structures they have created.

The hollow blocks which are much larger than the indoor blocks designed by Caroline Pratt are more appropriately scaled for use by the child directly and not through a surrogate figure. These hollow blocks are most often used outdoors, and it is here that we may see some of the same dramatic play from the classroom block scheme transferred to the outdoors. The group that has built a space center in the classroom complete with launching pad, gantry, controls, with rubber/wooden astronauts launched into space, when outdoors may build a larger space capsule from which they themselves may zoom off into space to find treasures and adventure in the unknown.

I recall, as a further example, a mixed age group of four-through six-year-olds who had built a block city. One of the buildings was a post office. The teacher took the group for several trips to a post office to add to their information. Following these experiences, the children returned to their block city post office with more understanding and details to be included. Yet their teacher sensed that they needed more direct reliving of their experiences. In this instance, the distancing through a surrogate figure removed them too far from the feel of what they were exploring. What developed was an abandoning for a while of the smaller, indoor blocks and turning to the use of hollow blocks indoors with which the children built a functioning post office which serviced several classrooms. Letters were written, notes delivered, packages mailed in a week of highly satisfying and exciting learning. Children need opportunities for both types of experiences, as they shuttle back and forth between stages of symbolization.

Connecting self and knowledge

It was proposed earlier that play may be viewed as the child's substitute for adult reflection, musing, hypothesizing. It is the child's way of bringing things together in order to find their relationship and connections while seeking clarification and understanding. The young child's task is to sort, order, and synthesize the information gathered from growing experiences in and interaction with the social and physical world. Information gathered in fragmented fashion is bent and turned to fit into the familiar. In some instances, like the peg which is too big for the hole, all the bends and turns do not make things fit and so the child must seek further in order to connect the parts and pieces. The same task confronts the child in terms of self—putting together feelings, fantasies, and reality. The child's understanding of self and the child's understanding of the world grow together and are intertwined.

In the joint activities of block building and dramatic play, the child is able to make several connections: (1) between self and knowledge by filtering new knowns through the backlog of experience; (2) within self through the imaginative activities which help to bring together feelings, fantasies, and reality. In this latter synthesis, the child combines the inner life of unconscious fantasy and the more accessible realm of known feelings with reality. It is only for the purpose of examination that this separation has been made, for within the person they are blended and interwoven. There are times when one part may predominate somewhat, subordinating the others, but there is invariably an interweaving that binds them together. It is in acts of imagination that a person is able to bring together in working harmony reality and fantasy thinking. Imagination will include reality because it is related to it, just as fantasy will include desires and drives because of their relationship.

The child has the opportunity to bring together reality and fantasy thinking in the imaginative activities of block building and dramatic play. The experiences of both realms are brought together in imagination and expressed in activity. As the child works at achieving a balance between fantasy and reality, play will often reflect the greater weight of one or the other. What is important in the activities of building and the play stemming from it is that the child is offered a *vehicle* for the act of balancing reality and fantasy. Too often the world of feelings, dreams, wishes is ignored by educators, which unfortunately leads to learning situations in which the child is only partially present, for what has been canceled is the engagement of the child's most personal self and her or his continuity.

If we value integration of self and responding to the whole child in a learning situation, then block building combined with dramatic play offers such opportunities for the teacher, just as these activities offer the child the opportunity to integrate information in the act of re-experiencing it. The re-experiencing becomes in itself an experience from which new connections may grow as the subjective and objective are intertwined, for in the doing the child wisely does not separate the cognitive and affective domains.

Expanding thinking style

From a 1964 Conference on Cognitive Studies and Curriculum Development held in the United States, I would like to present two remarks made by Piaget:

> The principal goal of education is to create men who are capable of doing new things, not simply of repeating what other generations have done—men who are creative, inventive, and discoverers. The second goal of education is to form minds which can be critical, can verify, and not accept everything they are offered. (Ripple and Rockcastle 1964, p. 5)

The question comes up whether to teach the structure, or to

present the child with situations where he is active and creates the structures himself . . . The goal in education is not to increase the amount of knowledge, but to create the possibilities for the child to invent and discover. When we teach too fast, we keep the child from inventing and discovering himself . . . Teaching means creating situations where structures can be discovered; it does not mean transmitting structures which may be assimilated at nothing other than a verbal level. (Ripple and Rockcastle, p. 3)

If thinking is to avoid stereotypic formulas, be critical and analytic in nature, and honor the originality and independence of the thinker, then the learning situations created to foster its development must model the very characteristics to be promoted. The "possibilities for the child to invent and discover" will certainly not arise in classrooms which inflexibly dictate the activities of the child, request the regurgitation of facts, limit the style of response, and which offer scant opportunity for the child's interaction and synthesis.

Learning situations must be sufficiently flexible and open-

An awareness of alternatives exists not only because play extends over a period of time which in itself creates opportunities for choices, but also because in a group a variety of interpretations becomes evident in interaction.

ended to permit the child scope both in thinking and activity. Such environments have been described in the wealth of books and articles on open education. Similar themes were examined and explored in great depth in the writings of John Dewey and other proponents of progressive education. Whatever the source, those learning situations which emphasize flexibility and open-endedness, viewed not as ends in themselves, but as consciously held values which will help promote independence, initiative, and inventiveness on the part of the learner, also tend to encourage divergence, experimentation, and analysis in thinking. Such an approach honors nuance, alternatives, choice, variety, doubt, freedom. This is the antithesis of a world of closure which has found all the right answers and in which there are few options, consequently leaving little, if any, room for self-discovery.

In block building and dramatic play, children have opportunities not only for self-discovery, but also the time and place where they may exercise the type of open thinking which has been discussed. To exercise choice is an ever-present option: *what structure is to be built, which role to play, how shall it be portrayed, which detail to add, which image selected, which emotion displayed, which interaction preferred, etc.* An awareness of alternatives exists not only because play extends over a period of time which in itself creates opportunities for choices, but also because in the group context a variety of interpretations becomes evident in interaction.

The *as if* nature of dramatic play is akin to the hypothetical moment. Without the pressures of time and consequence or a demanding reality, the child has the opportunity to toy with ideas and in such self-directed playfulness often discovers the new and original. Finally, in the creation of an *as if* situation, the child adheres behaviorally to the hypothetical premises stated and maintains a certain order to be followed within the social context of the group. This might be seen as a precursor of group games in which the child identifies with the group and adheres to its rules.

Role of the teacher

In connection with block building and dramatic play, what might be the role of the teacher? Thus far emphasis has centered on the child's role in self-directed learning and the opportunities which arise from use of the material and the activities which complement it. Earlier it was stated that it is the teacher who allocates space, quantity and variety of blocks, and supplementary materials. To this may be added: (1) the creation of the social atmosphere in which all occurs; (2) the adult's role as guide and/or catalyst in the learning situations which arise or are provided.

What does it mean specifically to act as guide, catalyst, and, to add another element, synthesizer? Examples may serve to illustrate these roles:

1. In a block scheme, a boy had built a fish store which he stocked by going fishing in the river (two blue lines painted on the floor across the width of the room which separated city from country). A girl went to his store to buy fish for her family and was told that the store was closed. Every time she went to his store he closed it. Finally, in great irritation, she yelled at him, "You can't do that. A store has to sell—that's what it's for, stupid." The teacher approached the children and entered the conversation first by listening and then in asking, "Can you go shopping in a store any time you feel like it?" Discussion led to the following conclusions: (1) you do not shop late at night because you have to sleep; (2) stores do have hours for shopping to which people must pay attention. (One tangential exchange on the last conclusion was "except for robbers, they can go anytime" and the exasperated response, "but they're not *shopping*, they're stealing.") It was decided that the boy and girl plus two other children who had joined the discussion would take a walk around the block with the teacher in order to find the answer to her question, "How do you know when a store opens and when it closes?"

They returned from their trip and as they entered the classroom, their newly gained information exploded: "It's on the door." "It's not the same for all the days." "They have a sign." Information was explored and shared. Signs went up on several buildings posting store hours. One child posted times for visits to her house, fixing the hours around the baby's sleeping schedule. To end this anecdote, and also to indicate that an inner agenda is not given up so easily, when the girl came back to the fish store and asked, "What *are* your hours?", the response was, "I'm open one day a week and today is not the open day."

2. Aside from other structures in the block scheme, there were a restaurant, a supermarket, and a farm. At the beginning of the week when these structures were first built, no connections existed among them. In the daily discussion time which preceded work in the block area, the teacher asked the children operating the supermarket where their fruits, vegetables, and milk came from. Taking the question literally, they responded, "We draw all the things and when we sell them all, we draw more." They were led to question where a real supermarket would get such items. "It comes on a truck." "The men put boxes on a long thing with wheels and the boxes go down to the cellar—whoosh!" "Vegetables come from the country because that's where the farmers are."

Following the introduction of her questions and the discussion, the teacher brought several books on farms into the classroom. Some children went on a trip to a small neighborhood grocery store. Over the week, some of the children continued this investigation. An immediate response to the discussion occurred in the block scheme. The children operating the restaurant went to the supermarket to get their soda supply. It was several block schemes later before any store owner from the city went to a farm to buy supplies. Actually, the beginning connection was made in a most delightful way. A boy who was working his farm became tired of waiting for other children to come and visit him so he took his cow from door to door in the city and sold milk on the spot.

Teacher functioning is not sharply delineated; invariably there is overlapping of roles. For example, in the second illustration, the teacher was both a catalyst in raising questions which were related to the children's activities, and also a synthesizer in that from her overall perspective of the block scheme she could lead children to finding connections both in their knowledge of reality and in their re-creation of it in dramatic play. The teacher wisely did not push her questioning past the children's interest or their ability to assimilate information. In this second anecdote, the children gathered most of their information vicariously through books and discussion rather than from direct experiences. Therefore, they would need more time and opportunities for understanding. Buying soda from a store was within the realm of their experiences; their experiences were then stretched to include another set of relationships among consumers—i.e., a store buying from a store. To see a connection between farm-store-restaurant was too abstract, and they could therefore not act upon it.

In the first example, we saw the teacher as guide leading the children toward resolution of their conflict, not by giving ready-made answers, but by bringing to the children's awareness factors which might be considered and offering the opportunity for discovery through direct experience. It might have been simpler to have stated, "Stores have regular hours. Let's make a sign that will tell people when to come to your fish store." By so doing, she would have deprived the children not only of the possibility for research and discovery, but also the opportunity to explore further the social aspects of the situation. Transferred to another material, it is the difference to be found between giving a child a jar of pink paint or in offering an empty jar and some red and white paint.

In observing children's buildings and the interaction in their dramatic play, the teacher may see where children are and what they have done with the experiences they have had. The teacher is offered a truly personalized opportunity, flexible and open-ended, in which to evaluate a child's learning. Within such an evaluation, the teacher may consider and plan for the next steps to be taken to ensure continuity in the child's experiences and learning. Cognizant of the child's level of development and experiences, the teacher in such planning tries to answer questions such as: *Does this child need more infor-mation or more time in order to proceed? How frequently has this child built a house? Has it been the same each time? Should I intervene? If I do, shall it be directly or by intro-ducing another child? Why is it that this child rarely builds a structure that can stand? At this moment, with this child, should I try to introduce more reality in the play? Or is this a time when I merely think about it and take no action—*

The teacher must exercise self-awareness and sensitivity toward others, and keep an open mind not only to the activities of children, but also to their vision and originality.

directly or indirectly? Why is it that when these two children build together, no matter what they start, it seems to end up as a jail? What kind of experience would be helpful to this small group trying to work out traffic patterns on the highway?

There are no ready answers or formulas. Each question must be answered individually in relation to a unique human being. What may be offered are a few general considerations such as: *How accurate is my observation? How well have I recorded—either mentally or in my notes? Is my question a reflection of something I am sensing rather than seeing? Can I pinpoint more accurately what I am feeling? What else does this child do during the day? Am I sufficiently aware of what this child's life is like outside of school? How do I balance this child's needs with my considerations for the group? On what am I basing my expectations?*

What is required of the teacher is that self-awareness and sensitivity toward others be exercised and refined, and that minds be kept open not only to the activities of children, but also to their vision and originality. What is offered to the teacher in the activities of block building and dramatic play is the opportunity to assist children in their search for clarity and understanding in a manner which is compatible to the learning style of the age and which activities directly connect to those feelings and interests which are relevant and important to the child. Dewey, writing in 1938 of the practices of progressive education, presented certain common principles which are appropriate to this topic:

> To imposition from above is opposed expression and cultivation of individuality; to external discipline is opposed free activity; to learning from texts and teachers, learning through experience; to acquisition of isolated skills and techniques by drill is opposed acquisition of them as means of attaining ends which make direct vital appeal; to preparation for a more or less remote future is opposed making the most of opportunities of present life; to static aims and materials is opposed acquaintance with a changing world. (1963, pp. 19–20)

Supporting the teacher's role

To what resources may teachers turn for assistance as they work with children in a block area? Questions, discussions, the reactions of other children all help to stimulate play, but there are also many times when a teacher senses the need for something else to support or spark play.

As was stated at the beginning of this chapter, for the young child there are few substitutes for direct experience. A young child will learn more from a real flower than from a picture of a flower. A picture may accurately record color, shape, detail, but it cannot capture what the flower smells like, whether the petals feel smooth or furry, or how it may yield to the wind. Yet there are many times when a direct experience is not possible, and so teachers must turn to other means to support children's learning. When books and pictures are used as sources, the teacher's job is to help the child to *connect* information gathered vicariously with that gained from direct experience. Some books are chosen because of their explicit, factual nature; others because they evoke mood and feelings. Similarly, a

teacher may put up a detailed picture of a bridge clearly showing span and towers and river banks, *and* a painting of a
bridge partially hidden by patches of fog, the illusion of twi-
light.

Still another opportunity both for guiding and sparking interest in blocks is through the use of props or supplementary
materials in play. These materials add those touches of reality,
the details, which help to give form to children's ideas. With the
exception of the rubber/wooden people and animals, colored
cubes and some transportation materials, batteries, and pulleys, most other supplementary materials may come from the
children's woodwork, the use of Plasticine, paper and crayons,
and all those things of which teachers are notorious
collectors—plastic containers, cans, egg cartons, empty spools,
pieces of cloth, wrapping paper, wool, string, etc. For example,
I recall the inventiveness of a child who built a beauty parlor
with five hair dryers under which sat five rubber people on
small square blocks. The dryers were made of small plastic
cups (collected from the weekly ice cream dessert) which had
been taped onto pillar blocks.

Choosing the type of supplementary materials to be used
raises the question of structured or unstructured materials.
*For example, in the block area, does the teacher buy the
small doll house furniture—beds, tables, chairs, television—
or are children encouraged to create their own furniture with
blocks or at the workbench? Does the teacher buy the sets of
traffic signals available in catalogs, or do children make their
own? The basic question is whether children are to be encouraged to use raw materials from which they may create
their props, or are children to be provided with ready-made
props for use?* In the unstructured, raw material aproach to
materials, the child's imagination is used to change form, and
to create. The child has the opportunity to make a personal
statement which may grow as the child's knowledge widens.
Ready-made furniture is static in the sense that it remains at
the level of the manufacturer's conception. With such materials, the child's imagination is used to put things together
rather than in changing form, creating.

Teachers may have a common goal for the children in their
classes, e.g., that they be able to create many of the sup-

plementary materials they use in block play from wood, string, paper, blocks, etc. What must be remembered in planning is that although teachers' goals create a framework for their functioning, the children of the class will differ in their ability to meet these goals. Some children will be able to meet the challenge immediately; some will follow the model set by other children and then act on their own initiative; others will need some teacher support and suggestions; and some children will not know how to function with raw materials. There are many children who, for a variety of reasons, find great difficulty in making that imaginative leap—to make something out of something—and who cannot proceed without a clearly defined, realistic base. In such instances, a teacher adhering to an unstructured approach may have to evaluate her or his goal with perspective. *Which is the ultimate goal: To have the child able to use blocks freely in building and dramatic play, or is the goal to create props out of raw materials?* If focus stays on the latter goal, then the whole might be missed by concentrating on a part.

For some children, unstructured materials cause a dilemma rather than serving the purpose of stimulating play. It is not unlike the blocked writer facing a blank sheet in the typewriter. For each, an opening must be found from which ideas may flow. For some children, *their* ideas cannot begin unless they have a realistic model and the direct and continued guidance of the teacher. With such support, openings are made possible. Unstructured materials provide children with greater learning opportunities than do ready-made materials, but they do also create difficulties for some children. It would seem that the task is not to alter the goal or destination, but to be aware that there are different ways of getting there. Dewey states:

> The teacher's business is to see that the occasion is taken advantage of. Since freedom resides in the operations of intelligent observation and judgment by which a purpose is developed, guidance given by the teacher to the exercise of the pupils' intelligence is an aid to freedom, not a restriction upon it. (1963, p. 71)

Blocks and primary children

In anecdotal material, illustrations have been drawn most frequently from classrooms of four- to six-year-olds. This is not to imply that this is a material restricted to these ages. On the contrary, the activities begun in these early ages, the budding processes described, may reach a fullness in the primary grades, which are marvelously exciting. Structures which may exist for a couple of hours for a four-year-old, a week with five-year-olds, may live on in the sustained, intricately planned activities of primary children for a couple of weeks. With older children, research takes on greater depth, and reality in itself becomes a moving force. A living city may grow, complete with battery-operated street lights, buzzing telephones, subway systems, and municipal government.

In one such scheme in which a group of children re-created aspects of their life in New York City, they brought the current events of the actual city—a milk strike—into the life of their block city. Information, ideas, and feelings about the milk strike were explored and clarified as the children re-created the strike situation in the block city and tried to find resolution for this conflict. Discussions and explanations grew out of their interaction with the issues as they participated in their re-created strike in a way which was not possible in the actual milk strike. It is not to be assumed that the children came to fully understand the complex political and economic factors involved in the strike, but they did reach a greater level of understanding than would have occurred had their involvement been solely on a verbal level. As Piaget has cautioned,

> This is a big danger of school—false accommodation which satisfies a child because it agrees with a verbal formula he has been given. This is a false equilibrium which satisfies a child by accommodating to words—to authority and not to objects as they present themselves to him . . . A teacher would do better not to correct a child's schemes, but to provide situations so he will correct them himself. (Ripple and Rockcastle 1964, p. 4)

As children move on to the middle years of childhood and beyond, the need to imaginatively re-create experience and to externalize feelings and thoughts does not diminish. A changed perspective, increased skills, and a firmer grasp on reality contribute to altering the forms of expression. What was experienced in dramatic play may now be transferred to the original, child-created plays which may grow out of social studies. Thus the child may continue to fuse knowledge, feelings and fantasy, breathing life and continuity into what is known. The child has come full circle to once again participating directly in play, but it is with an objectivity that was not possible earlier and from this vantage point views not only her or his knowledge, but also the cumulative process of self-identity.

Bibliography

Biber, B. "Play as a Growth Process." *Vassar Alumnae Magazine* 37, no. 2 (1951).

Biber, B. "Premature Structuring as a Deterrent to Creativity." *American Journal of Orthopsychiatry* 29, no. 2 (April 1959).

Biber, B. "A Learning-Teaching Paradigm Integrating Intellectual and Affective Processes." In *Behavioral Science Frontiers in Education*, ed. E.M. Bower and W.G. Hollister. New York: Wiley, 1967.

Biber, B., and Franklin, M.B. "The Relevance of Developmental and Psychodynamic Concepts to the Education of the Preschool Child." *Journal of the American Academy of Child Psychiatry* 6, no. 1 (January 1967): 5–24.

Dewey, J. *Experience and Education*. London: Collier-Macmillan, 1963.

Erikson, E.H. "Identity and the Life Cycle." *Psychological Issues* 1, no. 1 (1959).

Frank, L.K. "Play in Personality Development." *American Journal of Orthopsychiatry* 25, no. 3 (July 1955): 576–590.

Griffiths, R. *Imagination in Early Childhood*. London: Routledge & Kegan Paul, 1935.

Herron, R.E., and Sutton-Smith, B. *Child's Play*. New York: Wiley, 1971.

Isaacs, S. "The Nature and Function of Phantasy." *International Journal of Psychoanalysis* 29, Part II (1948): 73–96.

Isaacs, S. *Intellectual Growth in Young Children*. New York: Schocken, 1966.

Isaacs, S. *Social Development in Young Children*. New York: Schocken, 1972.

Johnson, H.M. *The Art of Block Building*. New York: Bank Street College of Education Publications, 1966 (first published in 1933).

Lowenfeld, M. *Play in Childhood*. New York: Wiley, Science Editions, 1967.

Millar, S. *The Psychology of Play*. London: Pellican, 1969.

Piaget, J. *Play, Dreams and Imitation in Childhood*. New York: W.W. Norton, 1962.

Piaget, J. *Science of Education and the Psychology of the Child.* New York: Viking, 1962.

Pratt, C. *I Learn from Children.* New York: Simon & Schuster, 1948.

Ripple, R.E., and Rockcastle, V.N., eds. *Piaget Rediscovered.* Conference on Cognitive Studies and Curriculum Development, Cornell University and the University of California, 1964.

Shapiro, E., and Biber, B. "The Education of Young Children: A Developmental-Interaction Approach." *Teachers College Record* 74, no. 1 (September 1972).

Sutton-Smith, B. "The Playful Modes of Knowing." In *Play: The Child Strives Toward Self-Realization,* ed. G. Engstrom. Washington, D.C.: National Association for the Education of Young Children, 1971.

Elizabeth Dreier

Blocks in the elementary school

Although viewponts in education may sometimes seem to swing with the pendulum of fashion, the most recent developments in the theory and research of human knowledge extend and deepen, but do not refute, the principal ideas of the philosophers who shaped modern education. That children need to be active and interactive learners—an idea expressed in the Deweyian phrase "learn by doing"—is confirmed in the burgeoning knowledge emerging from research based on Piagetian theory and on that grand compendium of disciplines known as human information processing (Bobrow and Collins 1975).

How young elementary children learn

Early elementary school age children are concrete operational thinkers who learn to understand the world by actively engaging with that world. They manipulate, investigate, explore, test, and change. They want to see what will happen if . . . . Through this interaction children take in the information from which they build an inner model of the world; they also build the intellectual structures which will enable them to take in and integrate more sophisticated information.

Piagetian insights into the intellectual development of children have led educators to wonder how much development can be fostered. Researchers have found little success in direct training methods, but there is a solid body of evidence that

153

indicates that social interaction among children working together to solve problems can help all of them to move to higher levels of intellectual functioning.

As a result of extensive investigation of the effects of social interaction on cognitive development, Bearison (1982) concluded that "Knowledge is not constructed independently of the social contexts in which it is shared, confirmed, and used to mediate social discourse" (p. 217). His subjects, working on problems in spatial perspective, were more successful when working in pairs and groups than alone. The differences in children's points of view raised questions in their minds and caused them to articulate and clarify their own views in the course of justifying them, and also to consider the views of others, which were often hotly defended. Sometimes the conflict resulted in completely new solutions not previously considered by either child.

Through the combined talents and efforts of psychologists and students of artificial intelligence and linguistics, we have learned that human memory is constructive, rather than replicative (Bransford et al. 1972; Bransford and McCarrell 1974). What we learn and recall to build on for further learning is the meaning we have made of our experiences, rather than a photocopy. People remember ideas, words, even images that they have never seen if these ideas and images represent the sense they have made of an experience, i.e., what they believe it meant.

It is not surprising then that *how* we represent in our memory what we have learned is a very important part of the learning process. Cognitive psychologists use the term *schema* to describe how we organize our world knowledge in memory (Rumelhart and Ortory 1977). A schema is a plan, a script, a scenario, perhaps a kind of play. It is not linear or simple, but complex and dynamic. Modern urban dwellers certainly have a schema for a restaurant. At its broadest level it prescribes food being served, a surface to put it on, a place to sit, and perhaps utensils. In reading this description, most readers will conjure up an image, rather vague, but containing tables, chairs, and perhaps waiters moving about, as well as some seated diners. If told that it is a Japanese restaurant, or a luncheonette, or a McDonald's, different, more specific, more detailed schemata will be activated. The reader will not have to be told that there are no tablecloths at McDonald's, nor that there are at an expensive restaurant. How are these schemata built, enriched, extended, and refined? The question is important because it is exactly this extension and deepening that constitutes learning.

Children in the elementary school years build these internal intellectual structures when they have rich opportunities to represent their ideas and new concepts in direct, concrete, physical ways, and when they have opportunities to manipulate, alter, and interact with the ideas through their representations.

Science and mathematics programs in the modern school often reflect these insights of Piagetian and cognitive theory in the provision of concrete materials and firsthand experiences as the essential tools for learning. How can we provide children with the opportunity for concrete interactions, for manipulation and investigation if the subject is social studies? Concepts are abstract, distances are great, time frames are large, events are often long past. This chapter will illustrate how blocks have singular potential for meeting this and other needs in elementary education.

Blocks in action

A class of urban second graders, having explored their immediate environment in kindergarten and first grade, were ready for a more systematic investigation that would enable them to organize their immediate experiences into the more abstract concepts of a city, and a more generalized understanding of the interrelationship of human functions within that city. Their block work was structured by the teacher. A rule was established that Block City would be real. Buildings must be of a kind that would be found in a city. Each child builder must find or make a person to represent her or him in the daily playing out of city life. Each daily session of block work was preceded by a class discussion, held in the meeting area, in which plans were made and many lively exchanges took place about what really happens in a city.

Children made accessories for their buildings, fleshing out

the basic materials supplied in neatly labeled boxes in the block area. Fruits and vegetables, all kinds of clothing, typewriters, stethoscopes, microcomputers, firehoses, pooper-scoopers . . . the list of needs that emerged during the semester's work was indeed long and varied. The materials used were many, and the methods inventive, as children made these objects from paper, wood, clay, fabric, and many found materials. They worked in shop and studio, as well as in their classroom.

After a day or two of work building time was declared over and all citizens of Block City engaged in the life and work that made their city go. On some days, the interests and curiosity of the children were sufficient to ensure lively interchange. At other times, when energy seemed to be low, or activities began to be repetitious, the teacher provided structure. There might be an assignment for the day: visit two recreation areas in the city, or buy two things today.

As these young children took part in the concrete representation of a process, questions arose that would not have occurred to them if their consideration of a topic had been only abstract. If all the people have to buy something in Block City, where will they get the money? The source of income for a shopkeeper quickly becomes evident, but how does the police officer get money? A second grade group working on this problem had many vigorous discussions, speculated on possible solutions, investigated through the library and through first-hand interviews, and was introduced in a meaningful way to concepts of city services, taxes, and interdependence in a society.

Another group, fighting one of the Block City fires that engaged the imagination of children moving out of the protection of early childhood and concerned about the safety of venturing away from Mommy, wondered how the water got into the hydrant that so readily supplied their hoses. The study that emerged from this question was extensive. It took them to the street to find and count hydrants and utility covers; to the reservoir to see the pumping station and interview the workers there; to the library to locate books, and read and be read to about the fascinating world under the city. They represented at least a dozen different kinds of pipes, cables, and conduits that carry the water, steam, electricity, phone lines, and other life-

The use of blocks to give physical form to their developing ideas enables elementary children to tackle complex problems, manipulate ideas, and integrate sophisticated concepts in mathematics and social studies.

lines of the city, giving reality and substance to the magic of light switches and faucets. This investigation led to many other explorations with water in the classroom—focusing on sinking and floating, on evaporation and drying. The city is a complex environment, too easily seen by children as magical. Processes, sequences, and cause and effect are difficult to observe. Block City makes them accessible.

The flexibility and appropriateness of blocks for supporting learning at many ages is readily seen in their use by nine- and ten-year-olds in another school whose curriculum included a much more sophisticated study of New York City for fourth and fifth graders. In learning about their city's history they modeled early New York, using many materials suited to the gabled buildings and cobblestone streets. When they began to study modern New York, they returned to familiar blocks, which seemed singularly suited to represent the bricks, concrete, and steel of angular contemporary architecture. They wanted to build Lower Manhattan to compare dramatically and in detail with their model of New Amsterdam. They also wanted to show the important features of "uptown" and, finally, of other boroughs. Much thinking went into solving the problem of representing such a quantity of information in the limited space of the classroom, while leaving some room for desks, chairs, and other more mundane but essential furniture. What a solid grasp of symbolization and the abstractions of mapping resulted from this exercise that engaged the imagination and reasoning powers of the whole class! They decided on a combination of realistic and symbolic representation—a solution appropriate to their transitional intellectual stage, and so important in helping them to make this intellectual step in a real rather than a superficial and superimposed way.

In their three-dimensional model Lower Manhattan was realistically represented, with detailed buildings complete to street addresses marked on their doors. Space and time did not allow this kind of representation of the rest of the city. So they mapped it, indicating major waterways, streets, and avenues, and represented with blocks the buildings and bridges they selected as important. Lively, often heated discussion centered on establishing criteria for importance. Gradually they moved from "my house" to "our school" to considering the services, supplies, activities, and functions essential to urban life.

"You have to have stores, silly, or there would be nothing to eat!"

"Well, but what about hospitals?"

"And movie theaters!" Like city councils, they debated the role of the arts in human life.

"Is the opera house important enough to include?"

"What about gas stations?"

"They're not important."

"Oh, yeah, how can the cars go?" And encountered the complexities of economic interdependence.

Little by little, the discussion turned to law and government. What really does go on in City Hall? They needed to know, to decide whether and how to include it in their city.

The final depiction involved symbols, a key, a scale, and a carefully worded indicator that the scale was different for the two parts of the model. This is a good example of the interaction between thought and action, between the growing capacity to deal with abstractions and the continuing need to ground such abstractions in concrete experience characteristic of school age children. Far from holding these children back, the use of blocks to give physical form to their developing ideas enabled them to tackle complex problems, manipulate ideas, and integrate sophisticated concepts in mathematics and the social studies.

Third graders became very interested in the river that ran next to their town. In their block area, they depicted the river, using blue paper carefully cut to follow its winding path. It took many walking trips to the local piers to give them the information they wanted about the neighboring town visible across the water, and then about the bridges that crossed their river. Their work led to many questions. Their dramatization of life in their Block Town awakened many interests. They built the warehouses and markets found along the wharves and furnished them with much produce and goods. They made boats with careful attention to detail. Their interest in and growing knowledge about the many kinds of boats that they saw in their trips led to increasingly elaborate woodworking. The children did not just make boats. They turned to books in the library for further details, so their models would have the authenticity that eight-year-olds want. This work led to much curiosity about where the cargo came from, and eventually to the making of a large map of the United States with symbols indicating the source of manufactured goods, food products, and raw materials that were brought to their community from around the country. This was a lesson in geography that had meaning and would be long remembered.

The same children wondered about the suspension bridge that spanned the river. While building it in block time, they noticed and speculated about the role of the suspension wires. Were they for decoration? What could they hold up, if they were attached to the bridge? And perhaps even more important, where could the answer to their questions be found?

The teacher added this question to the growing list kept on a large chart in the classroom. The group speculated about sources of information. One went off to the library to look under *B* in the card catalog.

"Try *S* for suspension," a classmate called after to him.

"Let's ask the man who owns the bridge," was another suggestion.

They learned about city government, about its departments and jurisdictions and sources of funding. They had first experiences in using their municipal services to obtain information, as citizens, and received a wonderful letter from the local bridge authority. Turning to more immediate sources for further information, the group visited the high school physics teacher's classroom, and received a classmate's engineer father as their guest. With what concentration and purpose they took notes—a first experience with this research skill! Finally, they built a suspension bridge and tested its load-bearing capacities with Matchbox cars. Were these lessons in civics? Physics? Language arts? Who is to say where such vital learning begins and ends?

Relationship of block building to the curriculum

Research and writing

The basic research skills of locating, organizing, and reporting information are difficult for many children. Teachers struggle to convey the complex skill of note taking. How do they know what to write down? Teachers struggle, too, to help children know what is meant by *putting it in your own words*. For many elementary age children it is hard to know how to decide what's important, and text is copied onto note cards because young researchers have no purpose of their own to guide their choice. We naturally put ideas into our own words when we have integrated the information. And human learners integrate what makes sense. So, to learn research skills, children must be engaged in a real quest.

Perhaps the biggest struggle centers on helping children learn to organize ideas in a report. This very abstract ability eludes and confuses many children. Two qualities make abstract experience accessible to school age children: purpose and a concrete referent. Representation of important new learnings in block building meets both of these criteria. Children seek information in response to their own, very immediate and concrete questions. In the beginning, these arise spontaneously, during block play, and the teacher is a major guide in the search. Quite quickly, children are able to use pictures in books, simple print, and the card catalog on their own. Because the children formulate the questions, they have little trouble knowing what is important. Because they want to hold on to the new idea, to report to their group, or to solve their own problem in blocks, they quickly learn to make a note or two. Because the notes serve their purposes, there is not so much confusion about what words to use, or what bit of information is worth recording. In such meaningful early experiences, children build a set of expectations about what research is all about. They do not see it as a school chore where the goal is to fill the number of note cards required by the teacher, according to some mysterious criterion. They establish a solid conviction that research is the meaningful quest for information for real purposes. Such children will begin soon to

Opportunities for writing and experimenting with scientific principles abound in the busy life of block cities.

establish some organizational principles of their own, and will see real sense in the formal skills lessons which are also necessary.

Current research in reading comprehension supports the view that most of the information used is in the mind of the reader (Kintsch and Van Dijk 1978). World knowledge, organized into schema, is essential to the reading process. Schema, or internal representations of events, objects, and ideas, are built and elaborated on by concrete operational children on the basis of real-world experiences. Complexity of association and vividness of experience determine the accessibility and sophistication of the schema.

Children in the middle grades begin to encounter abstract ideas in their content area reading. Concepts of government, economics, trade and barter, time and distance, properties of materials, and the functions of structures are all encountered increasingly in their texts. All of these concepts are exemplified in the block activities described here. The opportunities for the development of clear, personally meaningful, and elaborated concepts, or schema, to support the understanding of real abstractions will be limited only by the range and depth of topics studied through the medium of blocks. It is almost a cliché in education that children read and understand what is close to their own experience. Blocks are a way of bringing complex ideas about the distant and long ago world into the experience of children.

Opportunities for writing abound in the busy life of block cities. There are bookstores, libraries, publishing houses, and newspapers. One group of nine-year-olds produced sets of story books, carefully written in miniature. Another class published a block city newspaper, and decided that human size would be best. Events of the city were described, merchandise was advertised, and municipal problems were discussed in editorials. The class studied real dailies to learn about format and to see what kind of articles they could write. They stretched to cope with the reading level of their local paper, but it was worth it for such an interesting enterprise. Of course, their own newspaper required careful editing and proofreading, and these chores were rotated, so all had plenty of this valuable experience. Proofreading was done with a much more eagle eye than is commonly brought to such a chore. There were even arguments about the finer points of punctuation!

Scientific principles

Many practical problems in the building and use of a block city can be solved by the application of scientific principles. Buildings can be wired for electricity, and streets can be lit by a connected series of street lamps. The group that provided these utilities for their city used library skills, reading for content, and also much direct experimentation with bulbs, wires, and batteries before they were satisfied with the quality and reliability of their service. Ramps, pulleys, and levers are commonly devised and used, providing real understanding of the workings and purposes of simple machines, and a good beginning grasp of mechanics. Science in action of this kind is frequently seen in kindergarten block building, in early forms. Older children, carrying their investigations much further, encounter the need for systematic variation in their trials and for rigor in recording their findings. Their discoveries are more sophisticated and involve the elaboration of concepts that builds a solid foundation for classification, prediction, and hypothesis testing which are essential to later work in science, and to all clear thinking. In one school, five-year-olds were delighted to lift their elevator by pulling its string by hand through a simple pulley. Fourth graders wanted theirs to be raised by an Erector Set motor brought in by a classmate. The blocks were heavy for the limited power of the small motor, so they learned to rig a double pulley, and at the same time, learned a real appreciation of the relationship between distance, time, and work that underlies the usefulness of simple machines. How much more meaning the formulas that symbolize these relationships will have when they are encountered in high school physics! And how much less mysterious they will be!

Mathematical skills and concepts

Concepts of size and scale are worked through and developed in block building activities of all kinds. Beginners deal in broad approximations and consider notions of comparative size as they represent daily life. House furnishings and details such as doors need to fit the people who live in them. Cars and garages need to have a rough but appropriate proportion. These ideas are gradually refined through many experiences, much discussion, and some argument. Children in the upper elementary grades who have had such experiences are ready to deal with problems of size, scale, ratio, and proportion with precision and system. Grids that grow out of representations of city streets, often taped on the primary classroom floor, set the stage for solid mastery of both mapping and graphing, as coordinates are developed and used by young city planners. As always, the concrete referent allows the move to abstraction to take place with confidence and flexibility of application.

Children who have developed and used coordinates in response to real problems integrate truly abstract understanding of this and other tools, and have them available in their repertoire of problem-solving techniques rather than seeing them as the limited interests of the algebra teacher.

Buying and selling, and later, banking, provide many practical applications of computational skills. A fifth grade class moved into the study of percents earlier than their curriculum plan provided because they needed to compute interest in connection with their banking activity in Block City. Another group, somewhat younger, worked out a beginning understanding of percentage in order to hold sales in their shops.

Measurement is extensive and varied. Area and perimeter, height, weight, time, and distance are considered in real situations. Children gradually move from arbitrary units to precise use of standard measures. A common rule in early block building prohibits buildings taller than a child. Ingenious builders soon ask, "Which child?" and encounter the need for standard units. Older students devise more rigorous building codes, in response to the pressures of scarce space and the limits of building materials. They use rulers, yardsticks, meter sticks, tapes, and learn not only to use and read these tools, but also to choose the most efficient one for each task. Making lakes and swimming pools are examples of activities that have stimulated thoughtful consideration of problems of volume and capacity. A team charged with providing their town with a water tower realized that they had to consider the weight their tower would bear, and devised ingenious methods for weighing water, as well as computing the capacity of their container.

The role of the teacher

Because block building is so often thought of as a free choice activity for young children, teachers wonder what role they can and should play in a classroom block period for older children. The more experience the children have had with blocks, the more they benefit from structure and direction. Some of the areas in which structure for block use can be provided are described here.

Planning and discussion periods. All or most sessions of block use should begin and/or end with a group discussion. Topics can include planning for building; resolution of problems that have arisen during an activity period; assignments for the day; distribution of goods, services, labor, and materials; ways to find needed information; additional details or accessories needed; ways to extend the block city to incorporate the children's growing body of knowledge; record keeping; and many more.

Kinds of buildings. Young children can profit from sorting out reality from fantasy when asked to build only what can be found in a city. Older children can take part in decisions about what can and should be included. Is their city contemporary, or representative of an earlier time? Are buildings to be authentic? Shall there be more than one of the same kind? Are there limits on height? Size?

Topical focus. First and second graders, thinking in terms of how human needs are met in a city, may think with their teacher about buildings that are needed. Later, the teacher may choose a focus, for example: "This week all our buildings need to show how food is available in the city." Schools, hospitals, fire stations, and office buildings can demonstrate food sources. This project can spark thought, research, discussion, the production of many detailed accessories, and many questions for further study. In addition, it can produce interaction among citizens of the city, as, for example, the hospital staff plans how they will stock and staff their kitchen. For upper elementary children, the topical focus can be arrived at in group discussion, can be broader, and can serve over a larger period. "How are raw materials brought to our city?" In a class of nine- and ten-year-olds, each clerk can refer to this question, apply it to her or his own enterprise, do research to fill in information gaps, and plan with others to represent jointly the kind of transportation that will meet their common need to bring materials from a distance.

Numbers of children. The teacher has an important role in establishing guidelines about how many children can be involved in a project. In some classrooms, all children build and then live in a block city together. Much interesting interaction takes place, and the activity is given significance as a real tool for learning. In others, the teacher sees more benefit in the use of the area by teams or small groups, who then share with their classmates in a meeting. There may be one project seen to completion by a team, which is followed by another team, tackling another problem. Or, children may work in relays, on specific, assigned parts of an overall group project. Here is an opportunity for the teacher to see that all children gain experience with the extensive possibilities in the block area.

Rules for block city living. This is an area of great potential for moral development in children. Problems arise in blocks, as in any community. Space is scarce and needs to be shared. Commodities are not unlimited. "I need more doubles!" says one architect, who finds they have all been used. Another wants just the truck that a neighbor has found in the neatly labeled boxes stored on a shelf near the block area. Traffic poses as much difficulty to young citizens as to big city mayors! All of these difficulties are topics for group discussion. One class of seven-year-olds invented streets and zoning laws to control the chronic knocking down of buildings caused by congestion in their city. A grid was carefully laid out on the floor with masking tape, and a rule was decided on by the group limiting the number and size of buildings per lot. Ten-year-olds can generalize and categorize issues, and document solutions, for example, "Rules About Space" or "Sharing Materials," and amend and revise them.

Sometimes the solutions that children develop do not coincide with adult judgments. The teacher needs to be sensitive in deciding when to protect them from consequences which may be too much for them to handle, and when to let them live with and evaluate their own rules, and learn by doing so. Children who are active in developing rules have an appropriate understanding and respect for the meaning of laws. They see that laws are devised by human ingenuity in response to human problems. They can recognize that laws need not be arbitrary nor immutable to be blindly followed or as blindly bucked but can be creative approaches to felt needs, flexible and open to change in an orderly process.

Assignments. The teacher can ask each citizen of a block town, village, city, or other community to carry out a specific task in a given period of time. Young children may be asked to visit one friend or to go to two entertainments during a block period. Older children may have more complex assignments: getting a law passed; procuring the raw materials for a manu-

facturing enterprise; interviewing citizens or government offi-
cials for a newspaper article—all within the confines of their
block city.

Regardless of age, children beginning experience with blocks
go through developmental stages (see p. 193). Elementary level
children quickly reach or have already attained conceptual ability and skill in representing the real world in blocks as in other
materials. The teacher will want to see children using increasingly rigorous standards of reality, incorporating more detail,
including clearer sequential and logical representations of processes, and incorporating into their miniworld indications of
more abstract interrelationships. Children in the early elementary years are still moving out of an egocentric position. The
teacher can look for and support efforts to take into account
another's viewpoint, for example, "How will people in the city
know about the shoe sale?"

Children in the upper elementary grades are moving toward
more formal logical thinking. They will be increasingly able to
find symbolic ways to represent ideas and relationships. Now
they may make judgments about the salient features of their
city, abstract essential qualities, generate keys and other symbolic representations, and create constructions which are
models and three-dimensional mappings. Preadolescent children are approaching a time when they can consider hypothetical situations, and can be expected to demonstrate a beginning ability to draw on what they have learned of the real
world to construct a "what-if" world, and explore its implications. This is another example of the way concrete experience with blocks supports the growth of facility and power in
dealing with abstractions.

The teacher selects the kind of structure the group needs for
a variety of purposes: to promote interaction, to extend learning, to raise a question, to clarify thinking, to generate new
interest, to pose new problems for their consideration. Children give us cues concerning their interests, needs, misconceptions, and areas of readiness. Sometimes the most important time the teacher spends in block period is the time
spent quietly observing the children at work.

As children work in the block area, they are building in addition to cities, towns, rivers, and bridges an inner map of their

world. They are building a view of learning in which finding that something doesn't work is not a failure, but a cue to think and try again. They are learning the value of their own ideas and the courage to test them. They are learning the value of the ideas of others, and the confidence to consider them. Blocks have the flexibility that invites imagination, and the structure that requires respect. They afford children those opportunities that characterize the best education—the chance to venture and to reflect, to convince and to compromise, to wonder and to know, to reason and to dream.

Bibliography

Bearison, D. "New Directions in Studies of Social Interaction and Cognitive Growth." In *Social Cognitive Development in Context,* ed. F. Serafica. New York: Guilford, 1982.

Bobrow, D.G., and Collins, A.M., eds. *Representation and Understanding: Studies in Cognitive Science.* New York: Academic Press, 1975.

Bransford, J. D.; Barclay, J.; and Franks, J. "Sentence Memory: A Constructive Versus an Interpretive Approach." *Cognitive Psychology* 3 (1972): 193–10.

Bransford, J.D., and McCarrell, N.S. "A Sketch of a Cognitive Approach to Comprehension: Some Thoughts about Understanding What It Means to Comprehend." In *Cognition and the Symbolic Processes,* ed. W.B. Weimer and D.S. Palermo. Hillsdale, N.J.: Lawrence Erlbaum Associates, 1974.

Kintsch, W., and Van Dijk, T.A. "Toward a Model of Text Comprehension and Production." *Psychological Review* 84, no. 5 (1978): 363–94.

Piaget, J. *The Child's Construction of Reality.* London: Routledge & Kegan Paul, 1955.

Piaget, J., and Inhelder, B. *The Psychology of the Child.* London: Routledge & Kegan Paul, 1969.

Rumelhart, D., and Ortory, A. "The Representation of Knowledge in Memory." In *Schooling and the Acquisition of Knowledge,* ed. R. Anderson, R. Spiro, and W. Montague. Hillsdale, N.J.: Lawrence Erlbaum Associates, 1977.

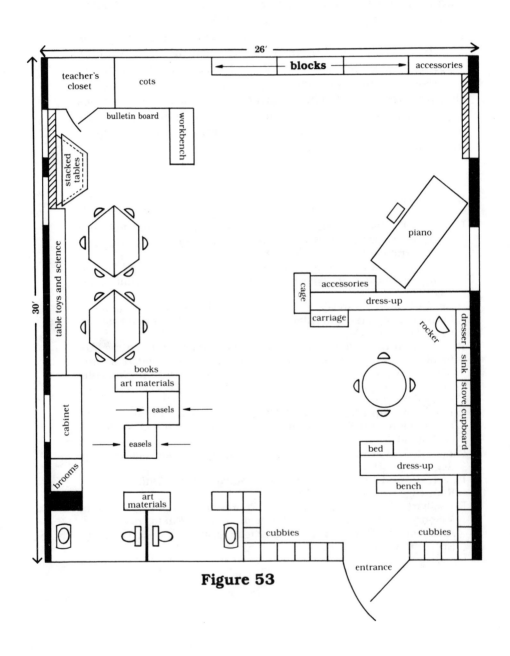

Figure 53

Elisabeth S. Hirsch

Block building
Practical considerations for the classroom teacher

Contributors to this volume have examined the various *whys* of block building activity. The practitioner, however, needs a *how* in addition to the why. This last chapter endeavors to relate theory to practice.

The physical space

Room arrangement

Nowhere is the adage "environment speaks to children" more appropriate than in relation to physical space available for block building activities. Block building needs a great deal of room. In an average classroom, about one-third of the floor space should be available for blocks. Of course, such space can be used for many other purposes at one time or another. It will be used for circle time by moving chairs or cushions; it certainly will be the area for music rhythm activities (although it might still be advisable to push other furniture aside at such

---

This room was the classroom of the four-year-old group at the Little Red Schoolhouse in New York City, where Elisabeth Hirsch taught for nine years. It proved to be a satisfying arrangement, allowing for a good flow of activity, and was easy to rearrange for meals, naps, and rhythms. Note the size of the block area.

Block building needs a great deal of room.

times); if the classroom contains a piano, it would be well to place it close to the block area. The area can also be used at other times. At mealtimes, tables and chairs that were pushed to the side or stacked during activity periods will easily find a place in the large block area. At naptime, cots can occupy the space.

Environment speaks to children. If a room is cluttered with tables (or desks) and chairs, it says *I want you to sit still, and control your urge to explore and to interact with people and things.* If the room is too large and undivided (like some church halls or gymnasiums), it says *run!* Children in such environments often feel abandoned. They miss supportive adult control. Their hysterical behavior shows that inner tensions have risen. It is difficult to achieve constructive, growth-promoting activities in rooms too crowded or cavernously spacious.

The block area should be large enough to provide room to build for all children who wish to do so. It is also desirable to have this area open, visible from other parts of the room. Fascinating patterns of interaction can develop between dramatic play areas, table toy areas, science areas, and the block corner.

In selecting the best area for blocks, the total traffic pattern needs to be considered. Block areas should be away from cross-traffic caused by the proximity of entrance doors or the bathroom.

In planning room arrangements experienced teachers usually select the block area *first*. The rest of the room will then be easy to arrange. The floor plan in Figure 53 shows one satisfactory solution.

Flooring

Any good, even flooring, free of splinters and away from drafts, is suitable for block building. Indoor/outdoor carpets (no pile) are certainly an attractive luxury in this area, as in any other part of the classroom. However, they are not vital. It should not be necessary to muffle the noise of falling blocks! A constructive classroom is a noisy place. Of course, accidents do happen and buildings do collapse, but in classes where children pile blocks upon each other in order to knock them down, constructive block activity does not exist. More about this later.

Shelving

Blocks need a great deal of shelf space. Three or four shelf units, each approximately 4 feet wide, 3 feet high, 1 foot deep, containing 3 shelves each, is probably the minimum required. Less will cause crowding (provided sufficient blocks and accessories are available) and make the blocks uninviting. More is certainly desirable. Shelving does not have to be expensive. Any handy carpenter can create good block shelves. (Specific suggestions for shelving will be found in Appendix 2.) Many teachers prefer not to have shelves attached to the walls. Judicious rearrangement of rooms is often the best remedy for mid-year doldrums. This is more easily accomplished with movable shelves. Movable shelves can also be used as room dividers wherever necessary. It is useful for some of the shelves to have vertical subdivisions. This allows for neater placement of various shapes and of accessories.

Blocks are expensive. With good care, blocks should last at least ten years.

Arrangement on shelves

Environment speaks to children. If blocks on shelves are too neatly arranged they say "don't touch." If they are too messy, they fail to suggest satisfying activity.

What is too neat? A shelf filled from top to bottom, from back to front, with identical blocks is too neat.

This is too neat!

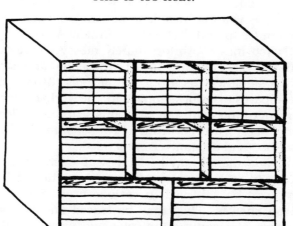

This is also too neat!

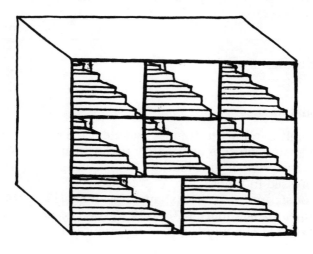

A shelf with identical blocks, where the bottom row reaches the front and the rest recedes in irregular steps, where the removal of a block does not destroy the entire design is, on the other hand, inviting.

A shelf where units or double units are arranged in such a way that their narrow end faces outward will be uninviting for another reason: builders will not be able to differentiate easily between half-units, units, and double units. They will be prevented from purposeful selection that furthers their work. Moreover, they will not be able to benefit from considerations discussed in Chapter 4, "The Block Builder Mathematician."

What is too messy? Unfortunately messy shelves need no description. They compare to a purposefully arranged block area in the same way as a box full of tools thrown in helter-skelter compares to a workshop where the worker can reach for neatly arranged tools without laborious searching. Block carts, boxes on wheels featured in many catalogs, invite the jumble just described and are not recommended.

Shelf arrangements may be kept neat easily, if the shapes that belong in each space are indicated on the shelf in some way. This can be achieved in various ways. Shapes can be painted on shelves. They may be traced on plain adhesive backed paper of a contrasting color and pasted on the shelf. Miniature shapes on the outside edge of the shelf itself might be helpful to older children. Younger ones might not be able to grasp the one-to-one correlation when one feature (size) is missing.

The Blocks

Sizes and Shapes

Although Caroline Pratt failed to patent the blocks designed by her, manufacturers fortunately retain the proportions and sizes of the original unit blocks. The following measurements are expressed in inches.

The *basic unit* is a brickshaped rectangle ($1\frac{3}{8} \times 2\frac{3}{4} \times 5\frac{1}{2}$). The *half unit* is square ($1\frac{3}{8} \times 2\frac{3}{4} \times 2\frac{3}{4}$). The *double unit* is $1\frac{3}{8} \times 2\frac{3}{4} \times 11$. The *quadruple unit* measures $1\frac{3}{8} \times 2\frac{3}{4} \times 22$. In addition to these basic shapes, there are quarter units, triangles, and ramps formed by bisecting a half unit, pillars, etc.

There is a great variety of other shapes combining straight and round surfaces such as arches of various sorts, cylinders, etc. These provide additional stimuli to block building activities. A recommended list of blocks for each age group will be found in Appendix 2.

Care of Blocks

Blocks are expensive. They are usually the most expensive equipment besides furniture. With good care, blocks should last at least ten years before they begin to splinter. Sanding can extend their lives even further.

Blocks should be made of hardwood, usually elm or maple. Softwood blocks are usually not durable enough for schools. They are too light and thus topple easily. They dent and splinter sooner and, in the long run, are more expensive.

Blocks will keep well if they are kept dry and free of dust. During long vacations, blocks can be kept in boxes or on their original shelves masked with newspapers or plastic. Occasional oiling, waxing, or shellacking will prolong block life considerably. This is a job that may well be done by teachers and children together. In addition to practical considerations, such an activity will also convey to children an attitude of appreciation for this material. Needless to say, blocks should not be used for other activities; for example, in lieu of a hammer in woodwork, instead of a rolling pin with clay, or in conjunction with water or sand.

Accessories

Accessories are indispensable to block activities. They can add stimulation, variety, beauty, and dramatic play content to block play.

The most useful accessories are: *human and animal figures*. These may be made of wood, plastic, rubber, or other materials. Other accessories include *cars, planes, boats, buses, trucks*—the list is virtually endless. Many of these items are readily available. Safety factors must be taken into consideration, of course. Sharp-edged tinny pieces can cause cuts and scratches. Another safety hazard is presented by soft cars (rubber or plastic) where the wheels are attached to rigid metal axles. These axles can cause puncture wounds when knelt on, for instance.

Interconnecting trains and interconnecting blocks are often popular and useful accessories.

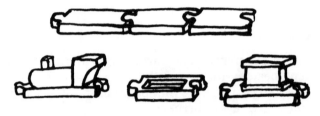

Another type of accessories is *decorations.* A finished building can gain further interest when the teacher suggests that it could be decorated. (See Appendix 2 for lists of accessories and suggestions for inexpensive and found materials that can enrich block play.)

It is worthwhile to note here that while accessories and decorations may be brightly colored, blocks should remain unpainted. Experiments with colored blocks have shown that they tend to restrict rather than stimulate imaginative activity.

If the room is arranged in such a way that the housekeeping area is near the block corner, the resulting interchange often enriches dramatic play in both areas.

A wise teacher does not display all accessories at one time. At the beginning of the year such wealth may be overwhelming. Reserves are necessary to pick up activities when they lag around mid-year. There should also be a reserve available to enrich special interests as they occur. Some odd-shaped blocks might also be kept for later in the year.

Other building materials

In many schools, large building materials are kept for outdoor use. Wooden hollow blocks and packing cases, ladders, sawhorses, cleated boards, etc., are standard equipment of many preschool play yards. If space permits, large-scale equipment adds an interesting further dimension to indoor play.

Relatively inexpensive hollow blocks made of corrugated board are usually reinforced inside and can easily support the weight of a child. These blocks have many uses. They can extend dramatic play activities by providing child-sized props. Their main disadvantage is that they are too light for high construction. There are other adverse features to consider. Cardboard blocks have a colorful patterned exterior which prevents rather than stimulates imaginative use. This exterior surface soon becomes shabby and worn looking. They lack what Harriet Cuffaro calls the "unitary harmonious nature of blocks" (see Chapter 6, p. 121).

Shortly before Caroline Pratt developed the unit blocks at the City and Country School, Patty Smith Hill developed another type of building material at Teachers College, Columbia University. Her ideas differed from those of Pratt: she did not want children to re-create their world, she wanted them to build an environment able to house dramatic play activities. She created building materials composed of interfitting planks and rods that were suitable for the creation of life-sized structures, houses, stores, etc. The original Patty Hill blocks have disappeared from the market; a number of companies are manufacturing equipment, however, embodying the same basic approach. While today's teachers will hardly want to decide on an either/or basis, they may find the large-sized construction units a very useful addition to classes for children of kindergarten age or older. Outdoor wooden hollow blocks in sufficient numbers can also be used for indoor dramatic play in the way envisioned by Hill.

Teacher concerns

Beginning activities

Parents who expect preschoolers to play with children their own age are always amazed when they watch beginning block activities. Children use blocks side-by-side, seemingly unaware of the presence of others. This is parallel play, a mode of activity which marks the beginning of block play at all ages and does not last long. Children soon become aware of the helpful or

Serious builders need to be reminded several times well ahead to finish up, because soon it will be cleanup time.

disturbing presence of others. At this point, when social codes have not yet emerged, when the activity does not yet provide real satisfaction, and when adjustment-time anxiety is high, teachers have to be especially aware of the block area. It is inevitable for young children, first entering a group, to become frustrated easily. It is, therefore, doubly necessary for the environment (including the teacher) to exert a calming influence. Teacher movement preferably should not be rushed and sudden. Shrill and tense teacher voice will affect children. The building area should be neat and calming. This is not yet the time to teach habits of neatness. It is unavoidable, in the beginning, for blocks to be scattered; for buildings to remain half-finished, or to collapse; for the area to take on a disorderly, uninviting appearance. It is wisest, at this time, for adults to pick up these uninviting (and hazardous) eyesores, while the children are still busy. Good cleanup habits will be easier to promote after playtime is over for the day.

Some preventive measures are also in order at this time. Without fail, children begin their buildings too close to each other or to the shelves. It is probably more effective at this point to move the building to a safe spot than to hold forth about rules.

The first rules that need to be introduced should probably have to do with respect for the activity itself—and for other people. "No, we can't knock down buildings. Let me help you take yours down." "It is dangerous to drive cars into buildings." "I can't let you throw blocks." No matter how we try to limit it, beginning group life is full of no-no's.

Role of the teacher

What if children don't use the blocks? There are a number of simple techniques that might encourage block play. The teacher's presence is one factor. A teacher sitting quietly in the block area soon has a number of builders around, especially in the early weeks of the school year. Another practice is derived from Gestalt psychology, which teaches us that people are bothered by unfinished tasks. Placing two double units at right angles in a conspicuous spot on the floor usually provokes some sort of block activity.

But the most important facilitator, of course, is the teacher's attitude. Teachers who value block building will find ways of transmitting those values in many ways, verbal and nonverbal. They will be available when blocks need to be shared. They will suggest a good place for building. Good teachers will provide moral support for fumbling artists. They will give suggestions, such as building a house or garage for a favorite toy or pet. They will stay with beginners, praise experimenters, and protect (or occasionally reconstruct) buildings. The activity (the process) is valued over the finished building (the product).

In the film *Incitement to Reading,* the teacher of a mixed first and second grade holds a morning meeting to help children decide what they will do first. Before all other choices, she asks for volunteers for block building. To those raising their hands she says "I'm glad you chose that." In the featured class, incidentally, the teacher had to choose between having desks or having blocks because of limited space. She chose the latter. The children consequently learn to read and write quite well lying on their stomachs, kneeling before chairs, as well as using conventional tables.

Rules

The teacher's role includes all facets of preventive safety. Sooner or later some rules have to be introduced—and enforced.

■ Do not walk on blocks (it is dangerous).

■ Blocks must never be thrown.

■ Buildings should be far enough from the shelf to allow others to get more (1–3 feet). (Painting or taping a line on the floor often helps to indicate the limit.)

■ Building height—this differs by child age and experience as well as by what teachers feel they can handle, but limits should be clearly understood.

■ Buildings should not be knocked, pushed, kicked down.

Let us remember though, that rules are made to help us, not to enslave us! There are times for exceptions to every rule. Children mature, teachers become more confident, individuals have differing needs. Children do not hold precedents against us. It is wise to avoid overreaction to infractions. It is usually better to be guided by the needs of the children themselves.

Collapsing buildings (accidental or otherwise), for instance, evoke panic reactions from children. They often throw themselves upon the pile with swimming movements. They seem completely overcome and, if no adult help is available **at once,** the sense of panic and highness can lead to even more loss of self-control. Many teachers find in such a situation that if they step in rapidly and pile identical-sized blocks three to four high right there on the floor, then the children will relax, carry the piles to the shelves, or even use them for new buildings then and there. The environment that seemed so threatening a few seconds before has become inviting again.

Once activities are well established and buildings become complex, the problem of whether to leave buildings up or not arises. There is no simple answer to this question once practical considerations, such as multiple use of space, do not interfere. The answer probably depends on the effect the leaving up of buildings will have. Does it convey to the children a respect for their effort? Does it stimulate extension, addition, improvement, decoration, or dramatic activity? Does it stimulate others to extend themselves by its example and by the appreciation of the adult? Or, conversely, does it discourage others, monopolize too much space, or use up so many blocks that there are not enough left for further activity? (In the latter case: does this class need more blocks?) Sometimes children clamor to leave a building up, but by next day they have lost interest. They were not yet ready for such an extended effort.

In rooms where buildings cannot be left up because the space is needed for another activity or another group, teachers sometimes have to help children over the heartbreak of dismantling. A sketch or an instant picture of a beloved building will convey adult appreciation, as well as provide permanency to an impermanent structure. Such pictures might serve as a basis for rebuilding the following day. They can also be exhibited for children and adults to admire.

Certainly no building should be left up because it is too much trouble to clear it away.

Cleanup

In some classes, cleanup time seems like a recurring nightmare to teachers. In others, it is a purposeful, busy activity enjoyed by all. How do we avoid the former and achieve the latter? It is necessary to consider some of the dynamics that cause the difficulties during cleanup periods.

An important consideration here is that of anxiety. While anxiety in minute quantities acts as a spur to investigation and creative activities, its destructive potential is enormous. A satisfying and busy activity period provides sufficient support to keep anxiety at bay. But transitions of any kind remove this support, and anxiety rears its destructive head. This is discussed more fully in *Transition Periods: Stumbling Blocks of Education* (Hirsch, n.d.). Feelings of insecurity, homesickness, and aggression surface; inner controls decrease. To alleviate these feelings, teachers can follow certain guidelines:

■ Cleanup should be a purposeful, satisfying activity in its own right, with enough time allowed for it to prevent rushing.

■ Children need a future orientation, i.e., they need to know what activity follows cleanup.

■ Confusion and destruction should be kept to a minimum. Knowing where blocks go provides a feeling of security. Having a teacher hand down the blocks from the upper story of a high building, thus avoiding collapse, prevents destructiveness. So does the quick response described earlier, should a building topple.

■ Waiting or inactivity makes anxiety rise. No child at any time during transition periods should be kept waiting, even if this means that some have snacks or go outdoors before everyone has completed cleanup. Children should know where to go once they are finished.

■ Clear expectation of purposeful activity and a follow through by actively participating teachers eliminates the feeling of helplessness.

■ Teacher help (and presence) also makes the task seem more manageable and more worthwhile.

There are a number of further points to consider here:

In some schools, the expectation is that "Everybody cleans up their own messes." Apart from the fact that important activities cannot be designated as messes, we have a further pitfall here: it is certainly easier to clean up some crayons and paper than an enormous block building. Block builders will soon assume that they have been punished. Block activity will fade. It is easier, then, to expect help from all in all areas to clean up *our* room. For some children, helping at cleanup provides the first acquaintance with blocks.

Some teachers give a prearranged signal (such as a chord on the piano) that suddenly announces *cleanup time.* While at the beginning of the year or in classes where the involvement level is low, this probably is quite effective; for serious, involved builders this is a frustration too hard to bear. Serious builders need to be reminded several times well ahead to finish up, because soon it will be cleanup time. The length of time and the frequency of reminders will vary with groups, age levels, and individuals. Teacher respect for individual activity, moreover, is expressed better by personal or small group reminders. Length of time for cleanup must be carefully scheduled and varied as the complexity of building activities increases. Cleanup time should be nonrushed and leisurely—it should not lead to inactivity and boredom.

The enjoyment of cleanup as an activity of its own will be enhanced if children have wagons and carts to deliver the blocks to the shelves. Some children pile the blocks on the chairs and push them to the shelves. If the area looks confused, piling up in twos or threes by teachers or children will again reduce confusion. In one school a teacher introduced first graders to mathematical sets by announcing that "Today we will put the blocks away in sets of two (or three or four)." Cleanup of this sort will produce its own patterns of cooperation and specialization. Thus we have important social factors at work here. Of course, teachers can and should be part of the team also!

Children who enjoy cleaning up begin building again while piling blocks on carts or chairs for delivery. The material is after all just too enticing! Teachers will have to use their own judgment on how to handle this in a not too discouraging way.

Just as in any other activity, children will test limits during cleanup. Here again, individual judgment must be used. We have to differentiate between testing and genuine need to do a little less on occasion. A hard-working builder might simply be too tired to clean up. Fatigue might be caused by other, less immediate reasons as well. Certainly cleanup should never seem a punishment, but neither should those who enjoy it feel that they have been had!

Since cleanup is often followed by toileting and washing hands, the two activities can go on simultaneously. Children can return from the bathroom to help further, if necessary. Such a flexible arrangement gives an easy "out" where this is indicated, without a clash of wills and bad feelings.

Other teacher concerns

Teachers are often concerned by the quality of the building activity. Some groups don't seem to graduate from flat, two-dimensional outlines to genuine building. Some groups seem to repeat other simple patterns seemingly forever. There is no single solution for any of these problems, since they often come from a variety of sources. Social leadership can be one cause. The most admired and imitated block builder is not always the most imaginative one. Teachers may consider ways of altering social constellations, or furthering other potential ideas. Sometimes this is the time for introducing some new accessories or for taking the group on an interesting trip.

Another problem is posed by tippy buildings. Equilibrium, balance, and stability are discussed in Chapter 3, "Children Learn about Science Through Block Building." It would be relatively easy to point out how buildings can be made more stable, but learning through problem solving will have more depth if children discover solutions themselves. Teachers will find that wise questioning often promotes better learning than showing how. Of course, here too there is no room for absolute purism. Sometimes teachers do have to give a hint or help with a technical problem and not worry that they have now stifled child thinking forever.

Children's concerns

Block building, like any other important satisfying activity, will help children gain skill in social relationships. Some children seem to have a natural endowment in this respect, while others face a very hard time. Teachers can help those with poor social skills by giving them specific suggestions on good ways to enter activities. ("Have you tried to bring them something they need for their building, like this horse?") Teacher disapproval of social discrimination will be conveyed in many ways and will discourage such practices.

In some classes, the block area seems to be a boy's domain and the housekeeping area that of the girls. Neither practice is rooted in children's nature, as clearly evidenced by classes where this segregation does not exist. Here again, teacher attitudes can convey that *all* children can enjoy these activities.

Classrooms where the block area is too small or insufficiently equipped force teachers to restrict the numbers participating in block activities. This seems rather regrettable not only because of the arbitrariness of the narrowed choices, but because it implies that children assigned to block play will have to stay in that area during the free play period. Children should have free movement whenever possible. Adjoining areas ought to provide cross-fertilization of ideas and populations. Involvement and attention length can only develop under conditions of free choice and commitment. When an area does become overpopulated, teachers could move furniture to accommodate those interested.

Aggressiveness and destruction

Adults are often concerned about aggressive children in the block area. Certainly, children have to be clearly aware of *do's* and *don't's* in relation to the blocks themselves. The reward in satisfaction is so great, however, that blocks are hardly ever used as weapons. Children with extremely weak inner controls will have to be very carefully watched of course and removed from the area if necessary. Some feel that such children should be allowed to knock down buildings, etc., for the emotional release this provides. Such an activity, while appropriate in a play therapy situation, is inappropriate and misplaced in a school. Schools should address themselves to personality strengths which they try to nurture and foster. Teachers can provide children who have weak inner controls with the control they lack by providing and enforcing safety rules. Impulsive or fearful children can often be helped in this way to feel safe, protected, and able to benefit from school activities. Most aggressive children relax and become less threatening once they feel safe. Safety for them means a teacher who protects them from their own impulsivity, as well as from outside threats, even if the protection means removal from the block area.

Children who bump into buildings, whether by accident or on purpose, are more common. They too need to be told that they are not yet ready to play in the block area. After a lapse of time, they will re-enter on probation. ("Are you ready to be more careful now?") Such accidents will occur less often if buildings are kept about five feet apart. It should be noted here that children who have such accidents frequently have problems relating to space perception or body image. Large-muscle activities such as those involving balancing are especially important for such children.

Differences in past experiences
of children

With the advent of Head Start and many more early childhood programs, many teachers who had over the years allowed middle-socioeconomic children to develop their own learning styles were heard to remark: "These children need more structure. You have to *teach* them how to use blocks." Is it possible that they were too impatient; that for lower-socioeconomic children, the school environment was even more strange, more threatening; that they needed a longer time for adjustment, than their middle-socioeconomic peers?

An experience in a New York City day care center makes us suspect that this might be the case. This new center was not yet fully equipped when it opened. Unit blocks were not delivered until six weeks after opening.

The teacher of one multi-age group reports the following:

On the first day that the unit blocks were in the room, W. (age 3) was the first to arrive at school. After discovering the blocks, he explored them tactually. He took a block from the shelf, held it in his hands, placed it on the floor and then replaced it and took another. After repeating this process many times, with blocks of different shapes and sizes, W. finally took a small cylinder, one that he found that he could hold easily, and walked around with it in his hand for most of the morning. Now, a month and a half later, he builds towers with the same cylinders, although he will run his cars over other peoples' roads.

G. (age 4), began by making upright ladders using the unit block, reaching about five or six levels high. He made several of these. Then G. sat on the floor next to his towers and systematically dismantled them. Using these blocks as he took them down, G. built a low three dimensional construction three or four stories high. Throughout his building, G. tried balancing blocks, experimenting with weight.

For about the first two or three days, play with blocks was entirely parallel. Boys as well as girls of all ages used the blocks. Most of the early buildings were of the ladder-tower variety.

On the fourth day, one child began to make a flat "road" and others joined in, each making his own road, almost oblivious of the others around him. During the second week, highway construction developed rapidly. Children began using ramps and also started to build elevated highways. (This was begun by a five year old and picked up by the others).

Socializing within the block area also began at this time. One day about four children built their own highways. As these individual highways grew, they became attached to each other and the children used this expanded road together. One child who had brought in several of his own cars from home, distributed them among the children in the block area. This too stimulated more cooperative play.

It was about this time that the teacher showed D. (a five year old), how a curve could be used in conjunction with straight blocks to make roadways turn gradually. He picked up the concept quickly, and together with his buddy, D. made highways using every curve available. However the other children continued to make straight roads.

During the third week, the children made a flat parquet type floor, subdividing it with partitions (double units). They then took out the wedgie people and animals and placed them in their stalls. The wedgies were used decoratively rather than dramatically. Up until this point, the children still had not built any kind of realistic building. Their constructions ranged from the most primitive type of tower to the more experimental type of construc- tions that I have mentioned. Various plastic accessories and wedgies were used for decoration rather than dramatic play.

During the fourth week, the first realistic structure was built. R. and A., two brothers aged four and five respectively, built a boat to which they continued to add pieces for decoration, a gun in the front, and people and animals were used dramatically.

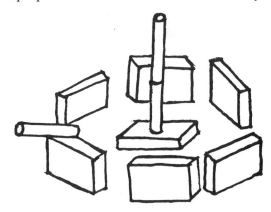

It has often been said that [low-income] children do not use blocks well because of their impoverished experiential backgrounds. And unlike middle class children, the[se] children should be shown how to use blocks.

These children did not seem to have any difficulty using blocks in creative ways; however, the blocks were introduced after the initial shock of the adjustment period was over. It may be that had the blocks been in the classroom from the very beginning, the use that the children put them to may not have been so good. Is it possible that [low-income] children coming into a middle class early childhood program, suffer a kind of culture shock, and that they are therefore unable to use materials to the best of their abilities in the beginning?

Observation by Susan Hirsch.

The foregoing is but one illustration of the difference children's backgrounds can make. Urban children will build differently from rural ones. Native American children will need to re-create experiences that differ widely from those of children in the hills of Appalachia.

Blocks and language

Some children are eager to discuss their buildings and explain various features. This is, of course,' to be encouraged, since language does add an additional dimension, a better ability to apply learnings another time, to the activity. Teachers who are sure they know what children mean to express may also supply the missing vocabulary. Talking about buildings becomes superficial, artificial, and can interfere with the process itself, however, if children are *expected* to describe their buildings. It is always better not to ask about a building *what is it?* but rather to inquire whether a child wants to *tell about it* if this seems indicated. Pointing out to others some special features, such as secure foundations, interesting ramps, etc., will gratify the builder, stimulate others, and build vocabulary.

Evaluation

The emphasis of this chapter is mainly on process rather than on product. It is implied that learning and growth processes are induced through the activity per se.

How, then, can a concerned teacher evaluate activity in a classroom? How does one know that an endeavor was successful? That children gain optimum benefit from block building activities?

The answer lies not in the *what* of block building, but in the *how*. If children work with an intensity that denotes satisfaction, we must be on the right track. What we are looking for is self-investment that encompasses the whole body, all senses, the intellect as well as the emotions.

Children just beginning their acquaintance with blocks are never fully involved. They are what one teacher called hit and run builders. Cleanup time is a five minute affair requiring no advance notice.

As the satisfaction provided by the material itself has an effect, things change: you can tell that children are involved by the noise quality in the room; there is a low, satisfied, busy hum in the block corner. You can see it by touching or looking at children's backs; there is a purposeful readying of muscles; this is not harmful tension, nor is it bored lassitude, this is a body at work. Look at children's faces: happy, busy block builders belie the stereotyped image of childhood; they don't laugh, they don't even smile—they are serious workers.

This is the point where the teacher who structured the room and the block area, who used psychology and diplomacy, who learned to bend and to kneel, to limit and to cajole, reaps the rewards.

Block building is worth it!

References

Hirsch, E. *Transition Periods: Stumbling Blocks of Education.* New York: Early Childhood Education Council of New York City, n.d.
Incitement to Reading. Film. Available from New York University Film Library.

Appendix 1

Stages of block building

This material is based on Harriet Johnson's *The Art of Block Building*. (An adapted version of *The Art of Block Building* appears as Chapter 2 of this volume.) Condensed by Maja Apelman.

It has been observed that whether children are introduced to blocks at the age of two or at the age of six, they seem to pass through all the stages (except Stage 1) described by Harriet Johnson. The only difference is that older children go through the early stages much more quickly and soon arrive at a stage more appropriate for their age.

Stage 1. Blocks are carried around, not used for construction. This applies to the very young child.

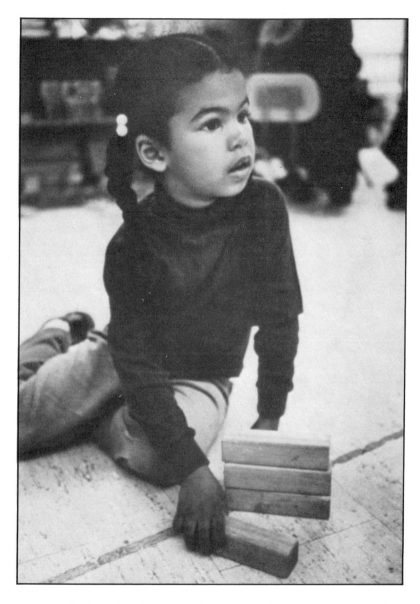

Stage 2. Building begins. Children make mostly rows, either horizontal (on the floor) or vertical (stacking). There is much repetition in this early building pattern.

Stage 3. Bridging: two blocks with a space between them, connected by a third block.

Stage 4. Enclosures: blocks placed in such a way that they enclose a space.

Bridging and enclosures are among the earliest technical building problems that children have to solve. They occur soon after a child begins to use blocks regularly.

Stage 5. When facility with blocks is acquired, decorative patterns appear. Much symmetry can be observed. Buildings, generally, are not yet named.

Stage 6. Naming of structures for dramatic play begins. Before that, children may also have named their structures, but the names were not necessarily related to the function of the building.

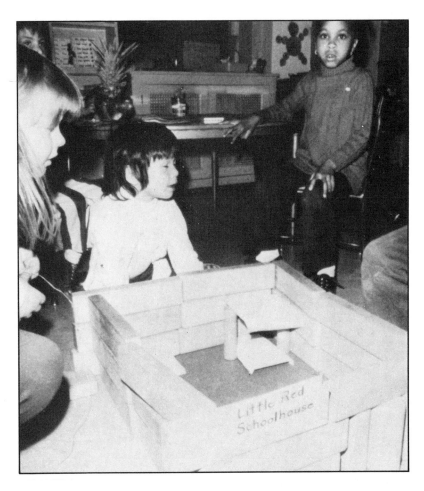

Stage 7. Children's buildings often reproduce or symbolize actual structures they know, and there is a strong impulse toward dramatic play around the block structures.

Appendix 2

Suggested equipment for block building

Set of blocks for a group of 15–20 children

(Numbers in parentheses refer to drawing.)

Number of blocks recommended for this age group

	3 years	4 years	5 years
Half units (1)	48	48	60
Units (2)	108	192	220
Double units (3)	96	140	190
Quadruple units (4)	48	48	72
Pillars (5)	24	48	72
Small cylinders (6)	20	32	40
Large cylinders (7)	20	24	32
Circular curves (8)	12	16	20
Elliptical curves (9)	8	16	20
Pairs of small triangles (10)	8	16	18
Pairs of large triangles (11)	4	8	12
Floor boards—11" (12)	12	30	60
Roof boards—22" (not illustrated)	0	12	20
Ramps (13)	12	32	40
Right-angle switches (14), and/or X switches (not illustrated)	0	4	8
Half pillars (not illustrated)	0	12	16
Y switches (15)	2	2	4

From *Play Equipment for the Nursery School* by Jessie Stanton, Alma Weisberg, and the faculty of the Bank Street School for Children.

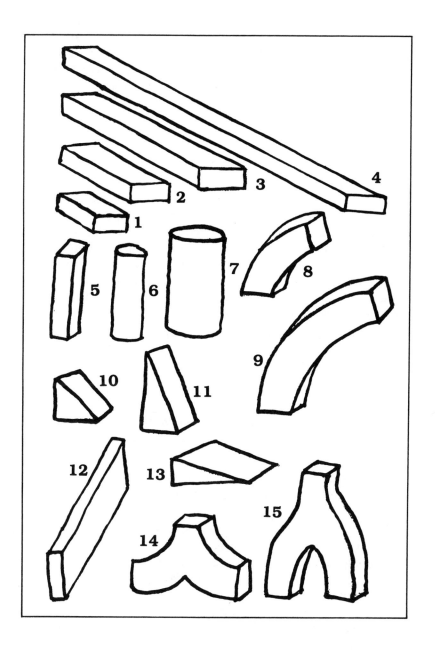

As children have more experience with blocks, greater varieties and quantities may be needed. Four-year-olds who have used blocks actively for a year or two, for example, will often use even more blocks than suggested for five-year-olds.

Block accessories

From Stanton, Weisberg, et al. (n.d.)

The suggested materials below demonstrate the range of materials children use to augment not only the block buildings, but their play with the structures. While the figures, animals, and vehicles are sufficiently varied to fulfill children's most recurrent themes, often the child's keen observation and commitment to realistic detail require other supplementary materials. There is often deeper satisfaction and a greater variety of imaginative themes when materials are suggestive of many uses rather than of a single function.

Rubber, plastic, or wooden figures (adults about 5" high)

2 varying ethnic families: mother, father, boy, girl, baby, grandparents

12 community figures: farmers, workers, doctors, firefighters, etc.

16 farm and domestic animals: cow, bull, calf, 2 horses, colt, sheep, ram, lamb, 2 pigs, piglets, cat, dog, etc.

1 set zoo animals

Vehicles (Plastic, rubber, or wood is recommended for younger children. Round-edged metal is safe for older children.)

2 sets trains and tracks (for older children), 2 sets interlocking trains or sandtrains (for younger children)

24 small cars, airplanes, buses, assorted trucks, and tractor (according to environment). Axles should be enclosed to prevent loss of wheels.

4 jumbo trucks (if floor space permits)

6 small and large boats (tugboats, barges, liners, ferries, etc., according to environment)

Additional accessories

Adapted from Maja Apelman, *Blockbuilding: Some Practical Suggestions for Teachers.* N.Y.U. Project Head Start In-Service Training Program. Mimeo. Used by permission.

Colored cubes are often considered part of the basic block accessories. Children love to decorate buildings with them. Any incomplete set of small blocks such as parquetry blocks or large dominos should be saved for the block corner. Also, any other assortment of odd small blocks or spools can be put into boxes for decorative use with buildings.

For five-year-olds and older:

Samples of tiles, linoleum squares, rugs with which children like to cover floor areas and walls of buildings and enjoy making decorative patterns.

Shells, such as scallop or clam shells: they can be used for plates when a child builds a restaurant (with food made of Plasticine) or again for decorative purposes.

Pebbles, small stones, little sticks for cargo on trains, boats, and trucks. Children can collect these on walks to a nearby park.

Variety of small containers is useful for all sorts of things, such as keeping money in a store, providing water for animals in a farm or zoo, etc.

Variety of lumber scraps, especially flat pieces for roofs, wide bridges, etc.

Furniture that is very simple and can be made at the woodworking bench. (Commercially bought furniture is either very expensive or very flimsy!) Children, however, should also be shown how to improvise furniture out of the blocks themselves.

Familiar signs such as one way, school crossing, bus stop, etc.

Tongue depressors for attaching signs, for making fences— they will stand up if stuck into a small piece of Plasticine.

Thin pieces of rubber tubing tacked to a cylinder block can make a simple gas pump. Children will think of other uses.

Excelsior makes good hay for farm animals.

Trees can be made very simply: let the child draw a tree, cut it out, then staple it to a tongue depressor and stick it into a piece of Plasticine so it will stand up.

Pulleys, with ropes and containers, make wonderful elevators.

Dry cell batteries with lights are popular.

Any old piece of machinery, especially if it has switches, or knobs that turn, can be placed in the block corner. An old TV antenna, a broken clock, earphones, or a radio will be used by the children in countless ways. Be certain to remove hazardous parts.

Save magazine pictures of bridges, roads, constructions, or city scenes and mount them on cardboard. Have them available for individual children who may need clarification when reconstructing something they have seen. Display them on walls of your block area if your layout permits this.

Children love to have signs written for their buildings. If these signs can be saved and stored in a simple manner, they can be used again and children may begin to recognize some of them. This is an excellent early reading activity.

Five-year-olds are very capable and independent. If Manila and colored construction paper, a few crayons, scissors, masking tape, and string are always available in or near the block corner, the children will begin to make their own signs, draw trees, people, and other things they need, and use their imagination in a constructive, purposeful way.

Note: The above lists are simply suggestions. Obviously, no teacher will ever put all these accessories out at once. However, the larger your supply of odds and ends, the better you will be able to help the children in the block corner when they begin to need accessories for specific purposes.

Block storage

From Stanton, Weisberg, et al. (n.d.)

Block cabinets should be sturdy, on a 3" baseboard, made of ¾" × 12" lumber, have a solid back, and should be divided into cubicles for orderly storage. The overall dimensions for a block cabinet for 15 three-year-olds might be 4'6" wide × 3' high.

Cubicles should be 11¾" high, with *small cubicles* (13" wide) for half units, cylinders, ramps, floor boards, pillars;

medium cubicles (18" wide) for trains, cube boxes, triangles, switches, curves, arches, small cars, and boats; *large cubicles* (24"–37" wide) for units, double units, quadruple units, roof boards, animals, people, other accessories.

Blocks should be presented in their shelves in such a way that their mathematical relationships can be perceived in terms of sizes and of categories of shapes. They should be arranged with the following considerations:

■ Large blocks and large vehicles should be near the bottom both for safety in removal and proper weighting of cabinet.

■ Each shape and type of accessory should have its own space for easier finding and orderly pickup.

■ The most popular shapes (units, double units, quadruple units) should be divided, where quantity is sufficient, to encourage building in front of different parts of the shelving. Younger children and novices tend to build immediately in front of the shelves.

■ Longer and lower cabinets (or two smaller cabinets) help in dispersing areas in which children build.

Reference

Stanton, J.; Weisberg, A.; and the faculty of Bank Street School for Children. *Play Equipment for the Nursery School.* New York: Bank Street College of Education Publications, n.d.

Contributors

Charlotte Brody, consultant, Day Care Unit, New York City Department of Health, was the principal of the Nursery-Elementary Division of the Little Red School House in New York. She has had experience teaching in and directing nursery schools.

Harriet K. Cuffaro is on the graduate faculty of the Bank Street College of Education, New York City. She taught at the City and Country School, the Child Development Center in New York City, and the public schools of California.

Elizabeth Dreier is coordinator of the Lower School of the New Lincoln School in New York City. Prior to that she was administrator at the Walden School and faculty member of The City College, City University of New York.

Elisabeth S. Hirsch is professor at the School of Education of The City College, City University of New York. She teaches courses related to early childhood education and child development. She has more than 20 years experience as teacher and administrator of preschools. She is author of *Problems of Early Childhood: An Annotated Bibliography and Guide* (Garland 1983).

Harriet M. Johnson came to early childhood education from a rich background in public health, teaching, and settlement work. In 1917, she planned an "educational experiment for young children" which she called "The Nursery School," one of the first in the United States. This school became the demonstration program of the Bank Street College of Education. Miss Johnson was the School's director and a Bank Street faculty member until the time of her death in 1934.

Kristina Leeb-Lundberg is professor at The City College, City University of New York. She has had experience as an instructor, teacher, consultant, and math specialist. She has worked with Dienes in Australia, Davis on the Madison Project, and Rosenbloom on the Minnemath team. She is an authority on Froebel.

Mary W. Moffitt is professor emeritus of Queens College, City University of New York. She is the author of numerous articles and books dealing with early childhood and science education. She was consultant on the film, *Blocks, a Medium for Perceptual Learning* (Campus Films, Tuckahoe, New York) and is author of the cassette tape-slide program "Block Building" (Childhood Resources).

Lucy Sprague Mitchell (1878–1967) devoted her long and productive life to the education of children and their teachers. She was founder and later president of the Bank Street College of Education. She was also the author of material for teachers in early childhood and elementary education and is probably best known for her milestone contributions to children's literature.

Charlotte Winsor, for many years director of the Graduate Program Division of the Bank Street College of Education, served at that college as archivist and Distinguished Teacher Education Specialist until her death in 1983. She was the author of many books and pamphlets and a teacher at the City and Country School at the time concepts of block building were originated and developed there.

Index

Information about NAEYC

NAEYC is . . .

. . . a membership supported organization of 40,000 people committed to fostering the growth and development of children from birth through age eight. Membership is open to all who share a desire to serve and act on behalf of the needs and rights of young children.

NAEYC provides . . .

. . . educational services and resources to adults who work with and for children, including

■ *Young Children,* the journal for early childhood educators

■ **Books, posters, and brochures** to expand your knowledge and commitment to young children, with topics including infants, curriculum, research, discipline, teacher education, and parent involvement

■ An **Annual Conference** that brings people from all over the country to share their expertise and advocate on behalf of children and families

■ **Week of the Young Child** celebrations sponsored by NAEYC Affiliate Groups across the country to call public attention to the needs and rights of children and families

■ **Insurance plans** for individuals and programs

■ **Public policy information** for informed advocacy efforts at all levels of government

For free information about membership, publications, or other NAEYC services . . .

. . . call NAEYC at 202-232-8777 or 800-424-2460 or write to NAEYC, 1834 Connecticut Avenue, N.W., Washington, DC 20009.